Karl Renner

Makers
of the
Modern
World

Karl Renner
Austria
Jamie Bulloch

HAUS HISTORIES

First published in Great Britain in 2009 by
Haus Publishing Ltd
70 Cadogan Place
London SW1X 9AH
www.hauspublishing.com

Copyright © Jamie Bulloch, 2009

The moral right of the author has been asserted

A CIP catalogue record for this book
is available from the British Library

ISBN 978-1-905791-89-7

Series design by Susan Buchanan
Typeset in Sabon by MacGuru Ltd
Printed in Dubai by Oriental Press
Map by Martin Lubikowski, ML Design, London

Contents

Preface: 'A Man for All Seasons'

Shortly before 11 a.m. on Wednesday, 10 September 1919, Karl Renner, several kilograms heavier than when he had first arrived in Paris back in May, entered the hall of the château in St Germain-en-Laye, which housed a museum of Neolithic exhibits. This was Renner's second visit to the Renaissance castle; on 2 June the French Premier Georges Clemenceau had handed him the Allied peace terms with Austria in this very same room. Now the Austrian Chancellor, and head of his country's delegation in Paris, had come to sign the treaty which would formally put an end to the war between the Entente Powers and one half of an Empire that no longer existed. The Habsburg Monarchy, which started the First World War with its offensive against Serbia, had disintegrated in the final weeks of the conflict. The representatives of the small republic of 'German-Austria' – as it wished to be known – pleaded in vain that their country could not be held responsible for the actions of the defunct Empire; the Allies insisted that somebody would have to pay for the devastation of the war years.

The terms to which Renner was about to put his signature were a slight improvement on those detailed in the draft Treaty.

But this was just a matter of degree. The Treaty was perceived to be excessively severe and had received a hostile reaction back in Austria. Renner, whose thick, greying beard compensated for the scarcity of hair on top of his head, nonetheless beamed as he took his place amidst the representatives of the Allied and Associated Powers, seated in a horseshoe arrangement in the hall. At a grand Louis XV table with a well-worn green leather top, Renner peered through his spectacles at the pens the Conference had provided for delegates, tested one on a spare piece of paper, and then signed his name with a flourish.[1]

'Dr Renner's cheerful acceptance of the treaty ... excited the admiration of all the allied delegates and spectators.'

NEW YORK TIMES, 10 SEPTEMBER 1919

The negotiations were over. Prohibited from entering into political union with Germany, and a shadow of its imperial self, rump Austria was condemned by the Treaty to live an independent existence, but seemingly without the material resources to do so. As the head of the Austrian peace delegation, Renner was obliged to shoulder much of the responsibility for the settlement; as Chancellor of the Republic he also had to return to Vienna and try to pick up the pieces of his shattered country.

Anton Pelinka, the renowned Austrian political scientist, has called Karl Renner 'a man for all seasons'.[2] He needed to be – Renner's life (1870–1950) spanned a turbulent period in the history of modern Austria, during which it underwent five separate political incarnations: (i) one half of the Habsburg Monarchy, (ii) the First Republic, (iii) the authoritarian 'corporate' state, (iv) an integral part of Nazi Germany, and (v) the Second Republic.

This volume is a biography of both Renner and the country

he served in a number of different capacities throughout his life. It begins with a short historical survey of the unique development of the Habsburg state and an outline of Renner's early life, from country boy in Moravia and gifted student in Vienna, to founding father of the First Austrian Republic. The second section of the book focuses in depth on the Treaty of St Germain, and Renner's dominant role as head of the Austrian delegation in Paris. The Peace Conference confirmed the new geo-political order in Central Europe resulting from the fragmentation of the Habsburg Empire in late 1918, which had a devastating effect on both the concept of 'Austria' and the material reality of the post-imperial state. The third section examines the aftermath of St Germain in Austria, and traces Renner's part in the unhappy history of the First Republic which plummeted into civil war, fascist dictatorship and then the Anschluss of 1938. Renner emerged unscathed from the Second World War, once again to found a republic and to play a leading political role in Austria, culminating in his election as President in December 1945. When he died five years later, the outlook for the Second Republic was far more auspicious than it had been for the First. The book will conclude with a consideration of how Renner's influence has shaped the political culture of post-war Austria.

Notes on nomenclature

1) The Habsburg Empire and Habsburg Monarchy (or the Monarchy for short) are used synonymously throughout. Austria-Hungary is also used to refer to the state as a whole from 1867–1918. For these 50 years of the 'dualist' era, Austria and Hungary refer to the western and eastern halves of the Empire respectively.

2) Out of personal preference, but also following a more

recent trend, the Habsburg rulers of the modern era, as well as the dynasty itself, are given their real (i.e. German) rather than anglicised names. Thus we have Franz and Karl, not Francis and Charles; Habsburg, not Hapsburg. For earlier rulers I have used the traditional nomenclature.

3) Given the multinational nature of the Habsburg Empire it is not surprising that many towns had multiple names in different languages. Where it has seemed appropriate I have given other versions in parentheses.

Karl Renner, his 'wife' Luise, and their daughter Leopoldine, around 1892. Karl and Luise did not formally get married until a few years later.

I
The Life and the Land

The Multinational Empire

A question of identity

In the period of Austrian history covered by Renner's life, a powerful engine of political development was the question of collective identity; successive generations of politicians had to tackle the problem of how to define 'Austria' and its relationship to the other elements in a Central Europe which was itself subject to profound change over the same period.

This was never more acute than in the wake of the resolutions of the Paris Peace Conference. The problem is perhaps most vividly illustrated by an observation made by a Liberal politician in the 1840s: 'Austria is a purely imagined name, which means neither a distinct people nor a land or nation. It is a conventional name for a complex of clearly differentiated nationalities ... There are Italians, Germans, Slavs, Hungarians, who together constitute the Austrian Empire. But there exists no Austria, no Austrian, no Austrian nationality, and, except for a span of land around Vienna, there never did. There are no attachments, no memories of centuries-old unity and greatness, no historical ties which knit the various peoples of one and the same state together – the history of

Austria is, all in all, small and sparse in factual material. None of these peoples is so much superior to any other in numbers, intelligence, or preponderant influence and wealth as to make it possible for any one to absorb the others in time.'[1]

Today, the 'span of land around Vienna' referred to above roughly corresponds with the two *Länder* (provinces) of Upper and Lower Austria. Back in the 12th century, under the rule of the Babenberg family, it constituted a duchy on the south-eastern fringe of the Carolingian Empire. The Habsburgs, who became Dukes of Austria in 1276, gradually acquired more territories in the region. These were generally won via shrewd marriage alliances rather than military conquest, giving rise to the oft-cited maxim '*Bella gerant alii, tu felix Austria nube*' ('Let others wage war; you, happy Austria, marry').

The marriage-broker *par excellence* of the Habsburg family was the Holy Roman Emperor Maximilian I (1459–1519). Through his first wife he acquired a large proportion of the Burgundian inheritance (including the Netherlands) for the dynasty. Then, by marrying his eldest son, Philip, to Joanna the Mad (the daughter of Ferdinand of Aragon and Isabella of Castile) he ushered in two centuries of Habsburg rule on the Spanish peninsula, which only came to an end when several generations of repeated in-breeding produced a king utterly incapable of fathering an heir. In Central Europe, Maximilian's most brilliant coup was to betroth Philip's two children to the offspring of the Jagiellonian King Ladislaus II. When in 1526 Ladislaus' son, Louis Jagiellon, was killed fighting the Ottoman Turks at the Battle of Mohács, Maximilian's grandson, Archduke Ferdinand, succeeded to the Bohemian and Hungarian crowns (including the Kingdom of Croatia).

The state complex of German, Bohemian and Hungarian lands which Ferdinand now ruled (a large proportion of Hungary in fact remained under Ottoman control until the late 17th century) formed the core of the Habsburg Monarchy for the next 400 years. And yet the totality of the family holdings lacked an official name. Ferdinand and his successors were, *inter alia*, Count of Tyrol, Duke of Styria, King of Bohemia and King of Hungary, but no title existed to denote the ruler of the sum of the kingdoms and crownlands. The fact that the sovereign of all these different lands was also Holy Roman Emperor – save for an intermezzo in the mid-18th century – perhaps obviated the need for a title to refer to the Habsburg lands collectively, or their ruler. Despite the problem of nomenclature, there was no denying the authority of this power in Central Europe which had risen to the top rank through its leading role both in the defence of Europe against the Turk, and in the Catholic Counter-Reformation.

On 11 August 1804, with the Holy Roman Empire on its deathbed, the Habsburg sovereign Franz issued a patent styling himself Emperor of Austria. Well aware that his existing title of Holy Roman Emperor had no more than theoretical significance, he wished to bestow upon himself the same dignity enjoyed by the Emperors of France and Russia. While the patent finally seemed to give concrete definition and cohesion to the entirety of the Habsburg lands, it in fact referred only to the Emperor and did not mention the name of the state he ruled. The term 'Austria' remained a designation of the Monarchy's ruling house, rather than a legal name for the Empire as a whole.

This lack of a collective name reflected the relationship of the various elements of the Habsburg Monarchy to each other. Although the territories were, for the most part,

THE HOLY ROMAN EMPIRE AND THE GERMAN CONFEDERATION
Voltaire (1694–1778) once quipped that the Holy Roman Empire was neither Holy, nor Roman, nor an Empire. His witty remark betrays the fact that it is difficult to give a precise definition to this amorphous entity which began life in AD 962 under Otto I and was dissolved by Franz II in 1806. Envisioned as the heir to the Roman Empire, but very much German, it was a collection of hundreds of principalities and free cities which, at its height, encompassed all of today's Germany, Belgium, the Netherlands, Austria (minus the Burgenland), the Czech Republic, Switzerland, Luxembourg, Liechtenstein and Slovenia, plus eastern France, northern Italy and western Poland. The Emperor's position at the head of this amalgamation of territories was weakened by the fact that it was, in principle, an elective crown; the Emperor was chosen by a small group of princes known as Electors. The first Habsburg to wear the imperial crown was Rudolf I in 1273, but from 1438 to 1806 the family provided all the Emperors, apart from a brief interregnum in the 18th century (1740–5).

For most of its history the Holy Roman Empire functioned as anything other than a unit, especially when the Reformation brought religious fragmentation, and thus provided individual rulers with the opportunity to challenge the Emperor's hegemony. For the last 300 years of its existence, the Empire battled on fairly impotently until Franz put it out of its misery. The German Confederation, established in 1820 as the successor to the Empire, was a loose association of German states, dominated by Austria and Prussia. It had its own federal assembly, and established a customs union in 1834 as a move towards economic integration. Rivalry between the two leading players intensified after the revolutionary year of 1848, climaxing in the Austro-Prussian War of 1866, as a consequence of which Austria was excluded from German affairs for good.

geographically contiguous, they were ethnically heterogeneous. What is more, they claimed their own rights and privileges based on past experiences of statehood. It sometimes appeared as if the Habsburg possessions were linked by little more than a common, powerful sovereign. It is true that the defeat of the rebellious Bohemian nobility early on in the Thirty Years' War (1620) destroyed Bohemian autonomy and brought the lands of the Bohemian crown under Vienna's sway. Moreover, the Pragmatic Sanction (a Magna Charta for the Habsburg Monarchy) issued by Emperor Charles VI early in the 18th century provided the Habsburg lands with a greater degree of political cohesion: for the purposes of succession, they were now to be treated as a single unit, i.e. they were to pass undivided from ruler to ruler. These constitutional developments notwithstanding, the Habsburgs were never able to achieve a lasting unitary, centralised state on the Western European model. Hungarian agreement to the terms of the Pragmatic Sanction was only obtained in return for recognition of its wide-ranging historic rights. When Joseph II (1741–90) made moves to centralise power in his dominions over half a century later, he ultimately came unstuck and had to rescind many of his modernising reforms. Later attempts in the 19th century to subject the dominions to central control from Vienna met with only temporary success and a good deal of resistance. Ultimately the Crown had to strike a bargain with Hungary, leading to the creation of the Dual Monarchy.

Prior to this settlement of 1867, 'Austria' was the conventional term for the Habsburg Empire in international affairs, and historians still employ this shorthand today, particularly in the context of war or diplomacy. But with the establishment of dualism, 'Austria' became 'Austria-Hungary' to the outside world, and remained thus until the collapse of the Empire at the end of the First World War. Internally, however, things were somewhat more complicated. One half of the Habsburg state was Hungary; that much, at least, was clear. But if you were a Czech or Italian with strong national sympathies, then there was no question of belonging to an entity (even half an entity) called 'Austria'. And, in fact, the western

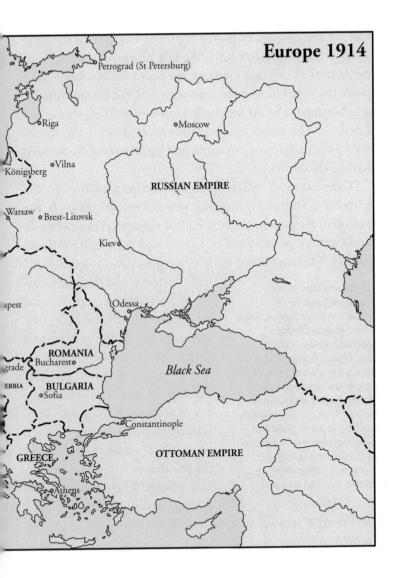

Europe 1914

Petrograd (St Petersburg)

Riga

Moscow

Vilna

Königsberg

RUSSIAN EMPIRE

Warsaw   Brest-Litovsk

Kiev

apest

Odessa

ROMANIA
grade   Bucharest

Black Sea

ERBIA   BULGARIA
Sofia

Constantinople

GREECE

OTTOMAN EMPIRE

Athens

half of the Monarchy lacked a proper name until the final year of the War, when Karl, the last Emperor, decreed it to be 'Austria'. Until that moment, the only official term used to cover the non-Hungarian territories was the extraordinarily cumbersome '*Die im Reichsrat vertretenen Königreiche und Länder*' ('The kingdoms and lands represented in the Reichsrat' – the parliament in Vienna that legislated for the western half of the Monarchy).

There were 11 officially recognised nationalities in the Habsburg Monarchy. Austrian was not one of them. In the 19th century and for the first half of the 20th, Franco-British and German perceptions of nation and nationality differed greatly. Whereas the one understood the nation as a geo-political construct, and thus nationality as an objective and political attribute, broadly speaking the other saw the nation as a cultural entity, tied up with language and ethnicity. A truly 'Austrian' identity in the late Habsburg era transcended national consciousness, suggesting instead an imperial patriotism focused on the dynasty and the Empire as a whole. When both of these disappeared in 1918, the idea of 'Austria' seemed to have lost all meaning and could not provide a strong basis for identification with the new republican state.

The 11 nationalities of the Monarchy, defined by an individual's mother tongue, were: Germans, Magyars (ethnic Hungarians), Poles, Italians, Czechs, Croats, Serbs, Romanians, Ruthenes (Ukrainians), Slovaks and Slovenes. Studies of the Habsburg Empire often divide these into 'historic' nationalities (those who at some point had enjoyed independent statehood – the first six in the list) and 'non-historic' nationalities (the remaining five who had not).

The Habsburg Monarchy in the 19th century

The Habsburg Empire which emerged a victor from the long Napoleonic Wars in 1815 was determined to stifle any revolutionary activity, both at home and abroad, which might once again turn Europe upside-down. Conservatism was the watchword, and it had the ideal figurehead in the Habsburg sovereign: Franz, the last Holy Roman Emperor and first Austrian one, was so averse to change that he made Prince Klemens von Metternich, his Foreign Minister and later Chancellor, appear almost radical. Yet Metternich, the colossus of pre-1848 Austrian politics, and a leading European statesman of the day, only countenanced reform where it might strengthen imperial power. Thus his sponsorship of cultural revival amongst the nationalities, and plans to reactivate the historical political institutions of the provinces – the diets controlled by local aristocracies – were strategies for bolstering conservative values; in other words, a 'divide and rule' policy.

Klemens Lothar Wenzel, Prince von Metternich (1773–1859) was the outstanding European statesman of his time. Born in the Rhineland, he moved to Vienna in the 1790s, became Austrian Foreign Minister in the wake of Austria's defeat by Napoleon in 1809 and presided over the Congress of Vienna (1814–15) which redrew the map of Europe after the defeat of the French. A conservative who liked to think of himself as a liberal, Metternich rose to become the leading politician in Austria. He was the architect of the system which bore his name and which was designed to ensure a balance of power amongst European states, as well as prevent another outbreak of revolution on the Continent. When his system came crashing down in 1848, he resigned and fled Vienna, but he returned in 1851 and continued to advise Emperor Franz Joseph until his death.

Metternich's scheme backfired, however: it fanned the flames of political nationalism rather than dampened them. It had been a mistake to believe that the Magyar (Hungarian) or Bohemian nobility would be satisfied with empty privileges which did not guarantee them real power over their own affairs. What was more, the national movements in both Hungary and the Bohemian lands were later overtaken by liberal reformers, and suddenly all this renewed interest in Slavonic or Magyar philology did not look so innocent. The Germans were not prepared to miss out either: as the most economically advanced of the Monarchy's nationalities, they were the foremost advocates of liberalism and constitutionalism. Moreover, the ranks of the bourgeoisie were swelled by the industrial expansion that took place in the first half of the 19th century, particularly the development of the railways.

Franz died in 1835. One of his final acts was to extract a promise from Metternich that nothing should change after his death. The new Emperor, Ferdinand II, was not as mentally incapacitated as most commentators have suggested, but chronic ill health, including severe epilepsy, prevented him from taking an active role in the affairs of state. Although he retained his title, real power was shared between Metternich himself and a handful of members of the imperial family.

The autocratic state that had stagnated under Franz came increasingly under attack from all sides. The touch-paper was lit by the demonstrations in Paris of February 1848, which led to the abdication of King Louis-Philippe. Metternich's nightmare came true and revolution spread through Europe. Vienna, Prague, Budapest and Venice were major flashpoints of revolt in the Monarchy. Metternich himself resigned in response to calls for his head, and fled Vienna disguised as a woman.

Everywhere, it seemed, the air was filled with talk of constitutional reform. The majority of the revolutionaries were not radicals aiming at tearing up the social fabric; rather, they wanted an end to autocratic and arbitrary government, an environment in which economic activity could develop successfully, and recognition of some basic national rights. Step by step, the revolutionaries extracted concessions from the Emperor, and various constitutional documents were sanctioned that year. In Hungary however, where a set of constitutional laws was approved in April, the programme became more radical and culminated in the War of Independence. The Hungarian uprising was finally quashed in August 1849 with the help of the Russian Tsar. Venice held out another week or so longer than the Hungarians; with its surrender, imperial authority had been re-established in all of the Habsburg dominions.

In December 1848, Ferdinand II abdicated in favour of his young nephew, Franz Joseph. This allowed the slate of the revolutionary year to be wiped clean; all the concessions of 1848 had been granted by Ferdinand. During the 1850s the Empire was governed by an absolutist regime, and Austria became a centralised, unitary state; any autonomy that the crownlands had enjoyed in the past – in Hungary this had always been pretty extensive – was abolished. Franz Joseph's subjects were denied representative government of any substance, and German was made the official language throughout the Empire.

Defeat at the hands of Napoleon III in 1859 brought the absolutist system to its knees. More serious was the equally unsuccessful outcome of the Austro-Prussian War a few years later. Prussia had usurped Austria as the pre-eminent German power and embarked on the process of unifying Germany. Austria, which had shared *de facto* leadership of the German Confederation with Prussia since the end of the Napoleonic Wars, was excluded from German affairs for good, and Franz Joseph was forced to come to some agreement with Hungary.

This resulted in the dualist settlement of 1867, which, as outlined above, divided the Monarchy into two halves: Hungary and the 'other lands belonging to His Majesty'. The only issues that concerned both halves were foreign and commercial policy, and the army; everything else was dealt with separately. Implicit in the settlement was that the Magyars would be the dominant nationality in their half of the Empire (they came to a separate agreement with the Croats in Hungary in 1868), while the Germans would run affairs in the western half. As Count Andrássy, a leading Hungarian statesman and one of the architects of dualism, is supposed to have said, 'You look after your Slavs, and we'll look after ours.'[2]

Renner's childhood

Such was the state of the Habsburg Monarchy when Karl Renner was born on 14 December 1870 in Unter-Tannowitz. He was either the 17th or 18th child of Maria Renner; as one of twin boys, nobody knew exactly. In fact, nobody ever knew whether this future Austrian Chancellor and President was indeed Karl, or his brother Anton. At birth, the former had been given a red armband, the latter a blue one. After the two boys had been baptised, the armbands somehow slipped off, got mixed up, and were retied after some hasty guesswork. Tragically, Anton – or the one who was then wearing the blue armband – died when he was only a few weeks old. As the future socialist Renner noted in his memoir, nobody could have foreseen just how appropriate the colour of *his* armband was to be in his adult life.[3]

So Karl grew up the youngest of a very large brood which spanned a generation; he was already an uncle at the time of his birth, and his cradle would often be rocked by a niece or nephew. Both his parents came from good German peasant stock. Renner's great-grandfather had moved from Saxony in the mid-18th century and settled by the river Thaya, which today roughly follows the border between Austria and the Czech Republic. It was an area blessed with fertile soil. Unusually for the time, this ancestor had been made a free man by his enlightened and generous master, and he was able to attain a decent level of prosperity which was maintained by his son, Matthias Renner (Karl's grandfather).

The family house, however, had been bought by his maternal grandfather. Karl's mother had first married Franz Zecha, who died young in 1851, and with whom she had three children (one of whom had also died in infancy). In 1852, she married Matthäus Renner, Karl's father, who by the time of Karl's birth in 1870 was focusing on the production and sale of wine, especially sacramental wine. He would spend weeks each year, in early spring and late summer, travelling from parish to parish in northern Moravia and Austrian, taking orders from the priests' offices.

The Austro-Prussian War of 1866 hit farming families particularly badly, as the hostilities – which involved harsh levels of requisitioning – coincided with a failed harvest, followed by a terrible drought. It seems as if Matthäus Renner, unlike his shrewd forefathers, was fairly naïve in financial matters. Like many peasants of the day, he had taken advantage of the increased availability of credit to expand his farm, and had also made some ill-judged investments in new agricultural technology. In the wake of the disasters of 1866, he was forced to mortgage his business at high repayment rates, and this was the beginning of a 19-year struggle to keep the farm. Although several good harvests followed, the stock market crash of 1873 caused the wine trade to implode. Meanwhile, overseas imports led to a drop in grain prices, giving a foretaste of the agrarian crisis that would hit Europe hard in the 1880s. In the year of the crash, the Renners sold off half of their house, and then gradually let go of field after field to service their debts.

Unter-Tannowitz lay in the south of the crownland of Moravia, which bordered Lower Austria. Along with Bohemia and Silesia, Moravia – birthplace of Sigmund Freud and childhood home of Gustav Mahler – constituted the historic Czech lands, or the lands of the crown of St Wenceslas. All these contained substantial German populations which remained until after the Second World War. More significantly, the economic and political muscle of the Germans was out of proportion to their actual numbers in the Czech lands, causing increasing levels of friction with the majority Czech population as they campaigned for greater national rights.

Although Renner grew up in a German-speaking enclave, he had ample contact with Czech people and their language, and by extension the multinational character of the Monarchy as a whole. This came primarily through an unofficial arrangement which the Renners had with a Czech family from Eibis (Czech: Ivaň), a dozen or so kilometres away. Boys from the two families spent terms living in each other's house, and so experienced a taste of life in a culturally foreign environment. Renner later regretted that he never had the opportunity to do an exchange, although he did spend a lot of time with the Czech boys who came to stay in Unter-Tannowitz. In addition to these guests, the Renner household frequently played host to groups of travelling performers or agricultural workers, many of whom were Czech, not to mention the Czech soldiers who would be billeted at their home when the Renners were in arrears with their tax payments.

Karl first went to school in the autumn of 1876. The liberal school laws from the previous decade had wrested education from the control of the Church and greatly expanded the provision of schooling in Austria. These changes, combined with the ambition of his parents for all their children to receive a proper basic education, helped the young Renner embark on his path towards academic distinction. He later commented that the local elementary school he attended was first class: in particular the tuition of both arithmetic and German was excellent. But his progress, initially, was quite slow. He was hampered both by the worsening poverty at home – the children were encouraged to look for stray eggs that they could sell to pay for books and stationery – and by a delicate constitution. Until the age of 12, Karl was short, skinny as a rake, and of such a nervous disposition that his hands would tremble when writing or drawing.

In spite of the disadvantages he faced, Karl managed to complete the eight stages of the elementary curriculum in five years. His teacher at the school informed the Renners that Karl was the most gifted of their children; he showed great academic promise and he must be permitted to complete his education. So Matthäus took his son to Nikolsburg (now Mikulov) to sit the examination for the town's grammar school. Karl passed, but the question remained as to how the family would afford the boy's board and lodgings. He failed to become one of the eight choirboys entitled to a free place. For a few weeks he stayed as a paying guest with the Nestrachil family, who had boys at the school. But the Renners soon found themselves unable to cover the weekly board for their son. One sad late October morning, Matthäus had to return to Nikolsburg to collect Karl and bring him home.

Karl immediately proposed a remarkable solution to the problem, one which reflected the 11-year-old's grim determination to escape his background of rural poverty: he would walk to and from school. On a fine day, when he was able to take a shortcut through the fields, this would mean an hour and a half each way. When the weather was not so clement, the round trip was closer to four hours. He kept this up for two whole years, and would occasionally meet colourful characters *en route*. He later wrote that these encounters gave him his first exposure to socialist ideas.[4]

During his first few years at the grammar school Renner was a fairly isolated figure. His humble rural background meant he had little in common with the boys from smart households in Nikolsburg, while the handful of pupils he knew from his village were all from richer peasant families. It was only in his third year that Renner really started to excel academically. He put this down to a succession of outstanding teachers, including Wilhelm Jerusalem, who later became Professor of Philosophy at Vienna University. But an additional factor from this point on was that Karl no longer needed to undertake the mammoth daily trek to and from school. In October 1883 he found a place to stay in Nikolsburg, with the widow of a forester who had been shot dead by poachers. The woman sought extra tuition for her two sons, and also needed help around the house. In return, Renner received free lodging and breakfast. Other meals were occasionally provided by some of the more affluent bourgeois families in Nikolsburg, who would offer free lunches to poor scholars.

The summer holidays were spent labouring on farms. Karl often went to stay with his mother's relations in Kunzendorf, a village in north-eastern Moravia where the Silesian German dialect was spoken. For Renner, this was a different world from the one he was used to in Unter-Tannowitz. In particular he noticed the difference in the food: an abundance of butter and bacon, and the novel experience of eating lentils and peas. In the summer of 1883, two months of agricultural work and an improved diet saw Karl shoot up and develop a much stronger physique – which meant he was unable to return home in the same suit he had worn on the journey to Kunzendorf.

The comparative affluence of his relatives put the wretchedness of Renner's parents' situation in sharper focus. In May 1885 the game was up: the family home was auctioned off, and his mother and father were forced to make the humiliating move into a poorhouse. By contrast, Karl was thriving in Nikolsburg. He had been offered lodgings in the house of one of the richest men in town, whose son needed intensive help with Latin and Greek. For half a year Renner experienced luxury on a scale of which he had never dreamed. This included several proper meals a day – with multiple courses – *and* a glass of wine at lunch and dinner. The mistress of the house also ensured he had good clothes to wear, and instructed him in etiquette, particularly with regard to eating. Renner observed that after only a few months he ate, dressed and acted as if he had been born into the bourgeoisie.[5]

Unfortunately, the son of this wealthy family made no improvement under Renner's private tuition. After six months Karl suggested to the father that his post ought to come to an end. He moved back in with the forester's widow, but then was awarded a grant from the provincial government of Moravia which would see him through the rest of his time at school. By now, Renner was also part of a group of friends who shared a passion for reading and intellectual enquiry. Tragically, his closest friend, Otmar Scherb, died of tuberculosis while still a schoolboy.

It came as no surprise when Karl passed his school-leaver's

certificate, the *Matura*, with distinction. After all, his Classics teacher at the Nikolsburg grammar school was of the opinion that even Cicero himself had not written better Latin than Karl.[6] At this point in his life, Renner had keen aspirations in the arts: he wanted to study philosophy and then become a poet and playwright. His next move would be to Vienna, fulfilling one of the farm boy's loftiest ambitions. He had already had a taste of the city when he went to stay with a friend who had left Nikolsburg a year earlier. Renner had been shocked by the decadent lifestyle of the students there, and resolved that he would spend his university years more judiciously. In any case, where would he find the money for the bouts of drinking and whoremongering he had witnessed on his short trip to the imperial capital? Now that his school grant had come to an end, Renner lacked the resources even to subsist as a student in Vienna. Not for the first time in his life he faced penury, and the path to a very promising career seemed to be blocked.

2
National Conflict

As the 19th century drew to a close, Austria-Hungary still ranked as a great power. With a population of 42.6 million in 1890, it was smaller than Germany, but larger than Britain, France and Italy. In international affairs its voice still counted for something around the negotiating table, and Bismarck clearly considered it a valuable ally, even if the last couple of Habsburg military outings had been anything but encouraging. Economically the Monarchy, especially the western half, had experienced a boom since the crash of 1873, and was no longer a predominantly agrarian state, although it continued to lag behind its more advanced Western European peers. Thus per capita Gross National Product was twice that of Russia, and greater than that of Italy, but only two-thirds of Germany's and France's, and less than half of Britain's. Per capita levels of industrialisation and other indicators painted a similar picture.[1]

Most male subjects of the Monarchy were obliged to serve for three years in the Habsburg army. As a scholar, however, Renner's term of duty was reduced to a single year, which he could choose to serve either before or after his university degree. His lack of funds ruled out study in the immediate term, and so Renner signed up for military service in Vienna in autumn 1889, which would allow him to gain a foothold in the city. He opted to join the field artillery rather than the infantry, as he supposed it would allow him more opportunity to exercise his brain and spend most of the time outdoors. His military service brought Renner into contact with Marxist theory for the first time, as well the entire spectrum of nationalities and social strata within the Monarchy. One of his comrades that year was a Magyar, with whom he engaged in intense debates about the rights and wrongs of Hungarian independence. These conversations sowed the idea of a political career in Renner's mind.

The dualist settlement of 1867 had given the Magyars the right to run their own affairs in the eastern half of the Monarchy, without reference to any government in Vienna. Franz Joseph remained the Sovereign – King of Hungary – and as such enjoyed wide-ranging powers, but he ruled through his royal ministers in Budapest. So long as no attempt was made to meddle in army affairs, which he jealously guarded as his own prerogative, he was generally happy to allow the ruling liberal elite in Hungary to pursue policies which aimed at reinforcing centralised control and assimilating the other nationalities and turning them into Hungarians, notwithstanding the settlement reached with the Croats in 1868.

Within the Austrian half of the Monarchy, the Germans were unable to sustain the same level of national hegemony, not least owing to the Sovereign's preference for a conservative rather than liberal administration. They also came up against an increasingly bellicose Czech opposition; the German-Czech conflict was to prove the most critical and damaging national struggle in Austria. The ultimate goal of the Czechs was to achieve a similar settlement to the 1867 compromise, whereby the Kingdom of Bohemia would form a third equal partner within the Habsburg Monarchy. On a more practical level, the Czechs demanded greater national rights, including an end to the 'electoral geometry' which gave the Germans a considerable advantage, and the raising of the status of the Czech language in the three crownlands as a language of administration and education. The Czechs resented the fact that only a few Germans in the provincial bureaucracies needed a knowledge of Czech, whereas they themselves were all obliged to be bilingual. Over the next half-century, the language issue raised its head time and time again – both as a real economic factor and as a symbol of national equality – without any lasting solution ever being found.

Constitutionally, Austria was made up of 15 crownlands, from the tiny Alpine Vorarlberg in the west, to the remote and fairly backward Bukovina in the east. Each of these had its own provincial diet (parliament) and administration. There was also a central parliament in Vienna, the Reichsrat, which comprised a House of Lords and a lower chamber, composed of representatives from the crownlands in proportion to their size. From 1873, the members of the House of Representatives were directly elected in each crownland (prior to that they were appointed by the provincial diets), which tipped the balance between the central government and regional ones in favour of the former.

In spite of this manifestation of popular political representation, the Sovereign retained considerable power. A democratic parliamentary election would expect to see the leader of the largest grouping appointed as Minister President. In Austria it worked the other way round. The Emperor chose his man first – almost always a member of the House of Lords rather than the elected chamber – and then gave him the Herculean task of securing a majority from the variegated factions in the lower house. Governments were fragile at best, and there was much chopping and changing over the years to appease the various groupings that had any influence, but the disarray produced by the system allowed Franz Joseph to keep a firm hand on government while maintaining the pretence of constitutionalism.

The broadening of his experience and contact with comrades of all nationalities were to influence Renner profoundly. He now resolved to study politics after his military service, and to grapple with the problem of the Empire and its nationalities. At the beginning of 1890, having grown frustrated at being stuck on the outskirts of Vienna, Renner jumped at the chance to transfer to the military provisioning store which was right in the city centre. Only a few months later he changed jobs again, becoming a full-time companion and tutor to a physically and mentally handicapped member of his company. This young man came from an influential military family, who were keen for their son to secure some sort of role for himself in the army. With Karl's help, the boy managed to pass his examination that September, which coincided with the end of Renner's 12-month term in the army.

Renner's talent for tutoring had afforded him an insight into a very different world from the one in which he had grown up. And had the prospective law student harboured ambitions to climb the social ladder, he may have taken the opportunity which now came his way. The mother of Renner's latest charge proposed that he should marry a 17-year-old friend of the family who was in disgrace after having given birth to an illegitimate child. Out of courtesy Renner agreed to meet the girl; he found her beautiful, intelligent and charming. But he declined the offer; in fact he was already in love with someone else.

Renner had enrolled at Vienna University in the autumn of 1890 to study law. While viewing some cheap, grotty digs, he bumped into a young girl called Luise Stoicsics, a serendipitous encounter which induced him to take the room. The two immediately fell in love. Renner had turned his back on the Catholic Church several years previously, and was also hostile to traditional marriage which he denounced as 'bourgeois'. Instead they held their own improvised ceremony in the presence of a few close student friends: Karl took Luise's hand and pledged to remain with her for life. From now on, he instructed his friends, they were to view Luise as his wife. The rapidity with which their relationship was put on such a permanent basis might cause the reader of Renner's memoir to raise an eyebrow; he neglects to mention at this point in his autobiography that Luise was pregnant at the time. So the birth of their daughter, Leopoldine, on 16 August 1891 comes as something of a surprise.

In fact, Renner was not around for the birth. For the whole of that summer he was engaged as a tutor to the 14-year-old son of Baron Bourgignon, the Deputy Governor of Lower Austria. This involved relocating to the rather sumptuous surroundings of Johnsdorf Castle in Moravia. Although Renner is keen, throughout his memoir, to emphasise his socialist credentials by underlining his abhorrence of big capital and inherited privilege – he asserts that working for affluent and propertied families tormented his conscience – he can barely conceal his enjoyment of the luxury he encountered at Johnsdorf. Typically for Renner, it was the food that made the greatest impression. He marvelled at the first meal he was served at the Castle: bottles of beer from the family's own brewery, trout from their own pond, venison from their own game park, and an array of magnificent desserts, cheese and fruit.[2]

It was a far cry from how others scraped by in Vienna. Renner was shocked by the wretched existence of some manual workers who lived in his district of the city. Rents for even the tiniest of spaces were inordinately high, leading to overcrowding and chronic homelessness. Renner used to give up his Sunday afternoons in an attempt to better such people's lives, either by reading to them from the German classics if the weather was poor, or by organising walks in the nearby Liebhartsthal. At all events, the idea was to provide the workers with an alternative to getting blind drunk in one of the nearby pubs, the traditional way of spending Sunday and the week's wages. This philanthropic activity brought Renner to the attention of the Viennese police, albeit in a rather curious way. One woman who was thoroughly irritated at having her lovemaking disturbed by whatever Schiller play Renner had decided to act out that afternoon denounced him to the authorities as an 'anarchist'. Although the police inspector who interrogated Renner had no other evidence than the woman's unconvincing testimony, Karl nonetheless found himself being trailed by a none-too-fit member of the secret police whom he was able to shake off with ease. A few days later his shadow disappeared for good.[3]

With finances very tight, Renner had to squeeze his studies in between the various jobs he could find. Luise also accepted a position as a housemaid, and so Leopoldine was put in care in nearby Purkersdorf, where her parents came to visit every weekend. It was not an ideal arrangement, and some commentators have seen the Renners' subsequent spoiling of their daughter as an attempt to expurgate the guilt they felt at having sent her away for a few years when she was very young.

Of course, care for the child involved further expense, and Renner also had to find the fees to pay for his law exams. So it was fortunate when he secured a position as a stand-in stenography lecturer at a private business school in Vienna. Although this work could be irregular, it was nevertheless very well paid, and by November 1892 Renner was earning enough to rent a flat for both him and Luise. Luckily, their landlord assumed they were a married couple and did not ask to see a wedding certificate.

Renner's active involvement with left-wing politics began around this time. The brother of one of his pupils belonged to a socialist cell at his school, despite being the son of a millionaire, and invited Renner to attend meetings in a small run-down pub called 'Zum heiligen Leopold'. Through this group he met figures such as the Austro-Marxist theorist Max Adler; the future German Finance Minister (Viennese by birth), Rudolf Hilferding; and Julius Deutsch, the future leader of the *Schutzbund*, the paramilitary force associated with the Social Democratic Party. Renner also discovered the works of Engels, whose *Socialism: Utopian and Scientific* made a particular impression on him.

Organised political socialism was still in its infancy in Austria, the Social Democratic Party having only been officially constituted at the turn of the year 1888/9. The young Renner was keen to get involved, and went to the Party's education headquarters in Vienna to offer his services as a speaker. Renner's talent was noted after some talks he gave in the Favoriten district of Vienna, and it was agreed that he should run a course on socialist theory. This was held from autumn 1894 to May 1895, and repeated a year later.

It was also at the education headquarters that Renner

first met Victor Adler, the founding father of Austrian Social Democracy. Less concerned with Marxist theory than others who would become key figures in Austrian socialism, Adler infused the Party from the beginning with a humanitarian spirit, together with a respect for the state and for law and order. Like Renner, he was motivated by a philanthropic concern for the poor and the oppressed. He observed Karl's eagerness for political involvement, yet advised him for the time being to continue working hard at his studies and secure a good middle-class job. While not losing touch with the socialist movement altogether, Renner should bide his time; the Party would call on his services at a later date when he would have far more to offer.

Three prominent figures of Austro-Marxism were called Adler, a fairly common German-Jewish surname. Victor Adler (1852–1918) was the founding father of Austrian Social Democracy and a representative of the moderate wing of the Party. His son, Friedrich Adler (1879–1960) was, by contrast, a radical. Friedrich assassinated Minister President Stürgkh in 1916, but was later pardoned. After the War he chaired the workers' and soldiers' councils in Austria, and then became Secretary-General of the Socialist Workers' International. The unrelated Max Adler (1873–1937) was a lawyer and social theorist who was also a member of the Austrian Parliament from 1920–3.

There was another obstruction to Renner's active involvement in party politics. A position as archivist had became available at the Reichsrat library in Vienna, and Renner's professor suggested Karl as his best student. Accepting the post would require him to make a pledge of impartiality, and would also shut the door on his prospective legal career. Karl found it a painful but unavoidable decision; seven additional years of practical preparation to become a lawyer were incompatible with his commitments as *paterfamilias*. Karl found a new apartment where he, Luise and Leopoldine could finally live together as a family. To afford this, however, he had to continue tutoring in the evenings, which did not leave much time for study.

The diligence and determination that Renner had shown as a schoolboy at Nikolsburg was, however, still very much in evidence. After several months as an exemplary government employee, he was awarded civil servant status, this in spite of objections raised at his 'living in sin' with Luise (the authorities were also a bit sniffy about Luise herself; in their opinion she was not Renner's 'equal'). In February 1897, however, the couple were officially married, and the following year Renner was awarded his law doctorate with distinction. With the Reichsrat library at his disposal, Renner now began to research and write monographs on legal, social-scientific and political subjects. Given the obligation to refrain from open political engagement, he published under a variety of assumed names.

The closing decade of the 19th century saw an intensification of the Czech-German conflict. What had looked like a successful attempt to achieve a language compromise under Minister President Count Taaffe in 1890, an agreement providing for the administrative division of Bohemia along national lines, was stillborn because only a minority of the Czech political elite – the more moderate faction – had been invited to the negotiations. The outcome was unacceptable to the more radical and numerous Czech party who wrecked the agreement. Violent clashes between Czech and German nationalists ensued, leading to the imposition of martial law in Prague in 1893. In 1897 Minister President Count Badeni issued a set of language ordinances that went far further in satisfying Czech *desiderata*. The new edict gave the Czech language the same status as German in large sections of the civil service throughout Bohemia and Moravia, thus requiring all state officials concerned to have a command of both languages. Given that far more Czechs knew German than the other way round, Badeni's ordinances put them at a great advantage.

In Bohemia the Germans took to the streets. Back in Vienna, Pan-Germans and German Liberals adopted a policy of obstructionism in the Reichsrat (beautifully documented by Mark Twain in a contemporary article).[4] When an attempt was made to exclude these two factions from Parliament, they were joined by Christian Socials and Social Democrats. Ugly scenes ensued in the Reichsrat, and police were called in to remove deputies engaged in fisticuffs. Demonstrations on the streets of 'German' cities became so menacing that Franz Joseph dismissed Badeni and ultimately rescinded the language ordinances. Of course, the U-turn only substituted Czech opposition for the German, but the Crown perceived this to be less threatening and more containable.

What made the Czech-German conflict so intransigent was a seemingly irreconcilable difference of opinion over the political structure of the Czech lands. The Czech nationalists obdurately stuck to the idea of the indivisibility of the Kingdom of Bohemia, whereas the Germans advocated an administrative partition of these territories into districts that were purely Czech, purely German, and mixed. Under this arrangement (which presaged the annexation of the Sudetenland in October 1938) no knowledge of the Czech language would be needed in the German districts; only in those areas impossible to divide up by nationality would bilingual training be required. As the Czechs rejected partition of any kind, they argued that their language should be on an equal footing with German throughout the Bohemian lands.

In 1899 Renner – under the pseudonym 'Synopticus'

– addressed the nationality issue in a tract entitled '*Staat und Nation*'.[5] Although the national groups in Austria enjoyed a constitutional right to equality, he observed, nowhere in Austrian law were the nationalities officially constituted as legal entities, i.e. they had no formal status. The crownlands did enjoy constitutional definition in Austria, and thus could be accorded various levels of autonomy or self-determination. But the problem in Austria was precisely that the individual crownlands were ethnically mixed, some much more so than others.

Invoking a formula that would resonate only too clearly in the Austria that would emerge from the Paris Peace Conference, Renner argued that the nation was a cultural rather than territorial concept. For this reason, he said, the national question would not be solved merely by identifying nations with crownlands. Using the analogy of the different religious denominations that had lived side by side in Austria since the Reformation, Renner pointed to how membership of the different denominations transcended political boundaries, and yet the churches were able to administer the affairs of their members irrespective of where they lived. The link between territory and religion had been severed, and thus the different congregations were able to co-exist peacefully.

In Renner's scheme, the nations – as legally constituted entities – would be personal associations rather than territorial entities. Each nation would have its own government or council, which would fund and administer the cultural affairs (including education) of all its members, wherever they were resident in Austria. In the political arena, the nationalities would vote for their own national candidates and be allocated a proportion of seats in the Reichsrat corresponding to the size of their national grouping. The same would hold true for posts in the bureaucratic apparatus of the state. By removing the conflict over public service jobs, Renner hoped that the nationalities would not object to using German to conduct business which affected Austria as a whole, as a pragmatic language of state. In other writings on the nationality struggle, Renner would develop his scheme of personal autonomy further; he devised a plan for doing away with the crownlands altogether, replacing them with eight *Gubernia* which better reflected the economic realities of early 20th-century Austria.

The Social Democratic Party conference in Brünn that same year also tackled the issue of national conflict. Given that the Party was a pan-Austrian organisation – it included Slav members as well as German – this occasioned much heated debate, and the resolution that was finally passed represented a compromise between German centralistic tendencies and Slav (particularly Czech) federalist ones. Ultimately the Party chose to cling to the idea of ethnic federalism, whereby the nationalities would constitute (as far as possible) homogenous territories. Renner's concept of personal autonomy as yet found no echo in the Social Democrat programme; for his part, Renner was critical of the concept of territorial autonomy, arguing that it would lead to violent domination of minorities.

Renner's approach to the nationality problem seemed vindicated when, amidst the gathering gloom of national antagonism within Austria, there emerged a faint beacon which perhaps pointed the way forward for the Monarchy. In 1905 a committee of the Moravian crownland diet worked out a series of bills which amounted to a compromise between the interests of Czechs and Germans. The new laws divided the diet into national curia, fixing the number of seats allocated to Czech and German deputies respectively. Each nationality would thus vote for its own politicians. The compromise also divided the Board of Education into national sections, and made provision for each municipality within Moravia to decide on the language(s) used by administrative bodies.

However, this positive development did not lead to a cooling of the Czech–German conflict in the main flashpoint, Bohemia, where the Germans constituted a larger proportion of the population than in Moravia. Bohemia was both a key symbol and heartland of Czech nationalism, and as such its historic rights would not be sacrificed merely for the sake of compromise. These considerations carried less weight in the more agricultural Moravia, where there was thus greater possibility for negotiation.

Meanwhile, another dynamic force was becoming entangled in the diversity of the Austrian political matrix. Up until the end of the 19th century, it was the national conflict that chiefly troubled the minds of Austria's political elite. The latter generally found that the only way forward was to play off the various factions against each other, in spite of the regular paralysis that resulted from such a strategy. The advent of socialism now added another dimension to political opposition in the Monarchy. It did, however, present the Emperor and his ministers with an opportunity to break the nationalist stranglehold on political life and so persevere with the policy of divide and rule. It would also present Karl Renner, one of the new MPs to be elected following franchise reform, with his entry into politics.

3

Twilight of the Empire

Renner was about to embark on his *Habilitation* – the post-doctoral thesis which qualifies an individual to teach at university – when an offer came from the Social Democratic Party asking him to stand as a candidate in the Reichsrat elections of May 1907. Although Renner had publicly kept his distance from the Social Democrats, he had remained in touch with the Party leadership all the while he was working in the Reichsrat library. Some doubted his suitability as a candidate; they believed his lack of a public profile would count against him at the election. But Renner's supporters pointed to his impressive output of political writings, and thus he was chosen to fight the constituency of Neunkirchen in Lower Austria, about 50 miles south of Vienna.

This opening into the world of politics was only possible thanks to a major constitutional change in Austria: the introduction of general and equal franchise. For a number of years, a succession of Minister Presidents had been toying with the idea of giving all men the vote. It was thought that the peasantry and industrial proletariat cared little for national emancipation; for these groups, social issues must surely take priority. By opening the floodgates, the hope was that democ-racy would swamp the rather elitist nationalist factions and render them harmless. In 1905 Franz Joseph had already threatened to introduce universal male suffrage in Hungary, where nationalist politicians were daring to interfere with *his* army. Faced with the loss of their social and national hegemony, the Hungarian political elite withdrew from the brink, and the bill for franchise reform was withdrawn. The Emperor kept the bill in his back pocket, however, should the Hungarians try anything similar again.

The Social Democrats had first contested Reichsrat elec-tions in 1897, for which the franchise had been extended, and had won 15 seats. At the 1901 election their number of deputies dropped to ten. With universal male suffrage now established in Austria, they expected to make significant gains at the May 1907 election. Renner was made to fight very hard for his seat. Nowhere in Neunkirchen were the Social Democrats permitted to hold a campaign meeting; one suspi-cious pub landlord after another turned them away. In spite of widespread anti-socialist prejudice, Renner triumphed, and the Social Democrats came away from the election with 87 deputies (50 Germans, 23 Czechs, 7 Poles, 5 Romanians and 2 Ruthenes) in a Parliament which had now swelled to 516 members. The largest grouping, with 96 seats, was the Christian Socials, a pronouncedly Catholic party that drew its support chiefly from the German peasantry and urban lower-middle classes. Originally a radical Viennese movement with a strong anti-Semitic element, the Christian Social Party gradually became more conservative and a bastion of impe-rial power. A total of 90 mandates were also won by various German-national groupings at the 1907 election.

As a new member of the House of Deputies, Renner

impressed almost immediately with his rhetorical skills, and he was elected onto several committees. He became an expert on budgetary and judicial matters, as well as on the terms of the 1867 settlement between Austria and Hungary. He was a fierce critic of the dualist structure of the Monarchy, as he showed in a debate on the quotas for the joint finances. In 1908 Renner was elected to the provincial diet of Lower Austria – which also convened in Vienna – of which he remained a member until 1921.

Meanwhile, Renner's writings on the nationality problems of the Monarchy had attracted the attention of leading Russian revolutionaries. The young Stalin called Renner's nationality programme 'an over-subtle form of nationalism', while Lenin attacked his principle of cultural autonomy. Trotsky was another critic. He had come to Vienna in 1907 after his escape from Siberian exile, and was not impressed by the lack of revolutionary spirit he found in the Austro-Marxist leaders overall. He stayed with Renner one night after an evening at the Café Central, and in later years dubbed him an 'operetta Chancellor'.[1]

If the founders of 'Austro-Marxism' tempered radical socialist doctrine with a commitment to democratic principles and parliamentary institutions, Renner himself seemed even less of a revolutionary figure. His earlier writings on the nationality question advocated a progressive social policy, but owed little to Marxist theory and more to the constitutional programme of the Liberals in 1848. At this time Renner was very pro-Austrian in his thinking, and dismissive of the idea of the nation-state as a blueprint for the future. Otto Bauer, the leading Social Democratic politician during the First Republic and the figurehead of the Party's left wing, agreed with many of Renner's ideas and developed them in his own work on the nationality issue. However, he criticised Renner for having underplayed – as he saw it – the importance of the social position of the working class.

Outwardly, too, Renner came across as anything but a revolutionary firebrand. His election to the Reichsrat and the Lower Austrian Diet finally provided him and his family with a decent income, and Renner eagerly cultivated the pleasures of bourgeois life such as cigar-smoking, for which he would become famous. In 1910 he also purchased, as his summer residence, a smart villa in Gloggnitz, near to his parliamentary constit-uency. And yet his association with the town extended beyond his status as a holiday homeowner; he would later establish a housing cooperative there, and he regularly organised excursions to the town as part of workers' education courses.

'I'm neither a reformist nor revolutionary; I can't be categorised as being on the Left or Right.'
KARL RENNER[2]

The democratisation of the electoral process in Austria had not brought about a democratisation of political life. It was never the intention that the Reichsrat should run Austrian affairs; not for one minute had the Crown contemplated relinquishing its grip on power. And yet the introduction of universal male suffrage suddenly saw the legislative process function far more smoothly. For a short period, Minister President Beck was able to work with a majority in the Reichsrat, and he even included some parliamentary representatives in his cabinet. But the hope that giving the vote to peasants and workers would dilute the 'bourgeois' nationalists ultimately proved naive. This was an era of universal primary education, and the lower, but literate, socio-economic groups were not, as had been supposed, immune to nationalism. Even the Social Democratic Party, which crossed national boundaries, did not remain unaffected. The fragility of the agreement upon which the 1899 Brünn programme rested became all too clear. When national questions were up for discussion in the Reichsrat, the various Social Democrat deputies voted with their nationality rather than as a unified party. Then, one month prior to the 1911 Reichsrat elections, the Czech Social Democrats founded their own party in Brünn. Following the election, which saw the socialists overall win a similar number of seats as in 1907, the Germans, Czechs and Poles all sat in national 'clubs' in the Reichsrat.

Karl Renner retained his seat in June 1911. As in the previous election, his campaign was a real struggle, so much so that Renner managed to forget completely about his daughter's *Matura*, the Austrian school-leaving examination. He was now a member of 32 specialist parliamentary committees and that same year was put in charge of the league of food cooperatives. In 1913, he joined the central committee of the International Cooperative Alliance. He was encouraged into this area by Victor Adler, and it would take up much of Renner's time over the coming decades, without ever bringing him much recognition.

Franz Joseph had dropped Beck as Minister President in November 1908 when it became apparent that the franchise reform was not the remedy for nationalism they had hoped for. From that point onwards Austria was governed with or without the consent of the Reichsrat, and a solidly German-centrist course was steered towards the confrontation that would destroy the centuries-old Empire. Ever since the humiliation of 1866, Franz Joseph had longed to regain some pride and assert the Monarchy's independence as a great power, even though it was the junior partner in the Austro-German alliance dating back to 1879. But when the chance

did arrive for the Monarchy to flex its muscles internationally, the very moment of its triumph also carried the seeds of
defeat. In 1908, Austria-Hungary formally annexed the two
Ottoman provinces of Bosnia and Herzegovina. Both had
been Habsburg protectorates since the Congress of Berlin
in 1878; now they were placed under the administration of
the ministry which looked after the finances pertaining to
the joint interests of Austria
and Hungary (the army and
foreign affairs). In this respect
they belonged neither to Austria,
nor to Hungary, but were the
only territorial expression of
the Dual Monarchy. Naively, the
Foreign Minister Count Alois
von Aehrenthal saw a Balkan
mission for Austria-Hungary
and briefly dreamed of carving
up Serbia between the Monarchy and Bulgaria. But the truth
was that the Monarchy could not
admit greater numbers of Slavs
within its borders while persist-
ing with an internal policy that
favoured Hungarians and Germans. Expansion only spelled
trouble. Confirmation of this arrived in June 1914 with the
assassination by a Serb nationalist of the Habsburg heir pre-
sumptive, Franz Ferdinand, in the Bosnian capital Sarajevo.
The Serbian Kingdom was handed an unacceptable ultimatum which would have made it a virtual client state of Austria-Hungary. The Monarchy knew full well that hostilities
with Serbia would bring in the Russian Empire and expand

The issue of Bosnia and
Herzegovina was part of the
larger problem, known as the
'Eastern Question', of what to do
with those Balkan territories
ceded by Turkey as it retreated
from Europe. The 1878 Congress
of Berlin – which revised the
treaty Russia had imposed on
Turkey after defeating it in the
war of 1877–8 – provided for
Habsburg administration of
Bosnia and Herzegovina, although
technically they remained under
the sovereignty of the Ottoman
Empire. Following the Young Turk
Revolution and Bulgaria's
declaration of full independence
from Turkey, Austria-Hungary
annexed the two provinces in
October 1908.

into a wider conflict. But it had been given a blank cheque by Germany to impose as harsh terms as it liked, and so the First World War was unleashed.

In spite of the levels of national discord within the Monarchy, the War was greeted as enthusiastically in the Habsburg lands as in the rest of Europe; the outbreak of hostilities in July did not immediately expose all the fault lines. For all the recent talk of South Slav brotherhood the Croats marched enthusiastically against Serbia, while the Poles had little problem in engaging with one of their traditional enemies, the Russians. Even the Italian and Romanian minorities, their national states not yet on the Allied side, performed their duty faithfully. The Czechs were predictably cooler in their attitude; for the first year at least, they refrained from outright opposition or subversion – at this stage it was still difficult to conceive of a future outside the Habsburg Empire. After initial protest the Social Democrats, too, were swept up by the bellicose mood. They professed their loyalty to the Monarchy and gave their support for a defensive war. Renner's patriotism went too far for the left of his party, however. His steadfast allegiance to the state leadership and interest in Naumann's *Mitteleuropa* plan, which envisioned German cultural and economic hegemony in Central Europe, was viewed with suspicion, and he was labelled a 'social imperialist'.[3] He fell out with figures such as the firebrand Friedrich Adler and the unrelated Max Adler, as well as with Rudolf Hilferding and others who began an ideological campaign against him, thereby breaking with the much-prized policy of party unity.

The initial assault on Serbia was an embarrassment for Austria-Hungary, which suffered massive losses. It was not until Bulgaria entered the War on the side of the Central

Powers in autumn 1915 that this small but determined foe was defeated. To the north-east, Russian armies overran most of Galicia in 1914, but they were pushed out the following year by combined German and Austro-Hungarian forces. A third front was opened when Italy joined the War on the Entente side in May 1915, having been promised generous spoils, most of which were Habsburg territory. The opening of the Italian campaign was welcomed by the Austrian military; here at last was an enemy they were confident they could vanquish, and not without some justification: none of the Italian offensives undertaken in 1915 were successful, encouraging the Austrian army to launch its own counter-offensive in May 1916. Austria broke through the Italian lines, but soon after had to withdraw troops to reinforce the position in Galicia. Its short-lived success was indicative of the fact that most of the best performances of the Austro-Hungarian army during the First World War were in the Italian theatre.

If the first two years of the War brought no great gains, at least Austria-Hungary had – albeit with considerable German assistance – managed to hold its own. Militarily, it was in a stable position. Internally, however, things were different. Italy and Romania's entry into the War (August 1916) severely diminished the loyalty of Italians and Romanians within the Monarchy to the Habsburg state. When supreme military command for the Central Powers was placed in the hands of the Kaiser – which meant Generals Hindenburg and Ludendorff – in late summer 1916, this only confirmed the suspicion of the nationalities that they were fighting a German war.[4] The Czechs had given vent to their anti-German feelings with mass desertions to the Russians on the Eastern Front, beginning in April 1915. There were numerous arrests of suspect Czechs and Serbs throughout this period. Under Tomáš Masaryk, a Czecho-Slovak council was founded in Paris, while a Yugoslav committee was similarly established in London. These groups of *émigrés* could not yet claim the authority to speak unilaterally for their nations, and any promises or assurances given by the Allied Powers at this stage were non-binding. But their voices were to influence future developments that would reorganise the political map of Central Europe.

At this stage of the War, a more serious challenge to the Monarchy's existence was the worsening food crisis. The Russian occupation of Galicia cut off for a period one of the Empire's most important granaries, while the British naval blockade and Italy's entry into the War greatly restricted the import of supplies from abroad. In May 1916, hunger demonstrations took place in Vienna. The prospect of radicalisation in Austria was made all the greater by the fact that the Reichsrat had been suspended since before the outbreak of war. In combination with harsh press censorship, this meant that there was no public forum for the articulation of political opposition. Rule in wartime was by emergency decree under Count Karl Stürgkh, who had served as Minister President since November 1911. Frustrated by this highly repressive regime, Friedrich Adler, whose earlier pacifism had turned into a tactic of terror, now resolved to assassinate a leading politician. He considered both Hungarian Minister President István Tisza (who in fact met his end at the hands of revolutionary Hungarian soldiers in 1918) and joint Foreign Minister István Burian as targets, but on 21 October 1916, he shot and killed Count Stürgkh, in the process disturbing the lunchtime sitting at the Viennese hotel Meißl & Schaden. At his trial in May 1917, Adler launched a scathing attack on Renner. He lambasted his party colleague for lacking principles and for disguising his 'real inner convictions' as an Austrian imperial patriot.[5]

In autumn 1916, Renner was offered a post by Stürgkh's successor, Ernest von Koerber, as director of the board that regulated the supply of cereals in wartime. He had recently come to the notice of government circles, as he seemed to be the one individual who might reconcile divergent factions in the Monarchy. After all, here was somebody who voiced his support for the War, advanced solutions for the preservation of the Empire under the Habsburgs, and yet as a Social Democrat had the potential to pacify the growing anger of the workers. In accepting the provisioning job Renner became the first Social Democrat to take government office in Austria.

On 21 November 1916, after an improbable 68 years as Emperor, Franz Joseph finally died. His reign had begun in the middle of revolutions which threatened Habsburg hegemony in Central Europe, and it ended only a couple of years before another wave of revolts dealt the death blow to a state that had lasted a whisker short of half a millennium. His time as Sovereign had seen a variety of experiments to solve 'the riddle of the Monarchy', as the nationality conflict was often called, but ultimately Franz Joseph stuck to the bargain thrashed out in 1867 which created the Dual Monarchy of Austria-Hungary. A whole host of other schemes were proposed, including Renner's principle of personal autonomy. Caught in a vice between an increasingly powerful Imperial Germany and the confidence of the Hungarian ruling elite, the Emperor never seriously countenanced any of these, thus ignoring the demands of his lesser nationalities and shying away from open conflict with the two 'master races' of the Empire. Although this gave rise to escalating levels of national tension, the prestigious figure of the Emperor himself provided an element of cohesion, a focus for if not patriotic sentiment then at least respect amongst all the peoples of the Monarchy. Without this glue the whole assembly of the Empire looked more fragile than ever.

Franz Joseph's successor, his great-nephew Karl, was 29 years old. Taking the throne at an unpromising time, lacking the necessary political training and known to be a more flexible man than his iron predecessor, he could only ever be the pale ghost of his many illustrious ancestors. Karl gathered around him a number of men who had been close to the late Franz Ferdinand, and who shared the latter's antipathy towards the Hungarians. But even had he been minded to bare his teeth at Budapest, Karl was in no position to do so, Hungary being in control of a large proportion of the Empire's grain supply. Instead, the new Sovereign was swiftly crowned King of Hungary, and swore the traditional oath to respect the Kingdom's laws and integrity.

Whatever Karl's aptitudes and shortcomings in reality, Renner was left unimpressed. The latter used his job as Director of Provisioning to secure an audience with the young Emperor, and planned to use this opportunity to discuss other subjects such as constitutional reform. He would also give Karl a copy of his new book, *Austria's Renewal*. But when the meeting took place at Laxenburg Palace, Renner was sorely disappointed: the Emperor was not going to allow this lowly official to talk to him about affairs of state. When Renner touched on the nationality question and presented Karl with his volume, the Emperor asked indifferently, 'Oh, so you've written books too?' Renner felt humiliated by the audience. When he left the room he lamented: *I don't believe the man even reads the paper … What a twerp!*[6] He later found out that Karl had thought he was a freemason and was afraid he might be a potential assassin.

In May 1917 Karl acted on his reformist leanings and the Reichsrat was finally reconvened. The deputies, who sat more tightly than ever in national clubs, had a lot to get off their chests after three years. Immediately, they set out national demands which exceeded anything they had articulated before. The Poles were the most uncompromising in their objectives. They would accept nothing short of a unified and independent Poland with access to the sea. The Ruthenes, meanwhile, sent greetings to their Ukrainian brothers in Russia, and voiced their goal of a free Ukrainian state. The majority of Czechs were for now slightly more cautious in their utterances, whatever they may have thought in private. Only a couple called for a new Czecho-Slovak state; the rest were content to attack the dualist system and demand the transformation of the Monarchy into a federation of free and equal states. The Slovene deputy Anton Korošec called for the unification of all Slovene, Serb and Croat districts of the Monarchy in an autonomous, democratic state under the Habsburgs.

At that same sitting Renner spoke out against past mistakes and the excessively authoritarian nature of the wartime government. He warned that if the Monarchy wished to survive it would have to prove its worth to all the nationalities. He also demanded the restoration of all freedoms to the people in Austria. In an attempt to scrape together Reichsrat support, Count Clam-Martinic, Austrian Minister President at the time, needed to broaden the composition of his government. In June 1917 he offered Renner a ministerial post as the Social Democratic representative in a coalition cabinet. The Party was resolutely against the idea. Fortunately for party unity, so was Renner. In other circumstances he might have found the proposition enticing, but he did not think very highly of Clam-Martinic, an arch-conservative from the Bohemian feudal aristocracy, and so was able to bow to the will of his Party without regret.

By the end of 1917 the Social Democrats, encouraged by revolutionary events in Russia, had shifted noticeably to the left. Otto Bauer returned from wartime imprisonment in Russia in September, and his star seemed to be ever rising as Renner's was on the wane. At the party conference in October – the first the Social Democrats had held during the War – the entire leadership was criticised for its loyal attitude towards the imperial government. Renner attracted particular censure from the left, as he was generally considered the most faithful Habsburg loyalist amongst all Social Democrats, the man who stuck to the idea of the supra-national Monarchy when all others had abandoned it. He defended his position at the conference, insisting he was a pragmatist, and it took a considerable effort from Victor Adler to prevent a split in the party.

On 11 November 1917, the Social Democrats organised demonstrations in favour of peace. At the conference they had passed a resolution echoing that of their comrades in Germany, which called for a peace without annexations or reparations. The Central Powers were still in a reasonable military position. Although the United States had declared war on Germany (not on the Monarchy, however), it would still be some time before it would actually be able to deploy troops and equipment. Then in October, Austria-Hungary achieved its single greatest victory in the War when, reinforced by German troops, its army broke through the Italian lines at the Battle of Caporetto, and advanced over 60 miles into the

Veneto. Meanwhile, events in Russia were rapidly making its war effort negligible; on 15 December the Bolsheviks signed an armistice. But no crushing victory could compensate for the poor harvest of 1917 following a drought that summer. In German and Hungarian districts the yield was half of what had been expected; in Slav districts the figure was one-third. Combined with a harsh winter that arrived early, the internal situation was highly volatile. A wave of strikes broke out in January 1918, protesting against a reduction in the daily flour ration. It was clear that Austria-Hungary would not be able to last another winter of war.

The Allied Powers began to declare amongst their war aims the autonomy or independence of the Poles, Czechs and Slovaks, and South Slavs, thus giving great impetus to their individual movements and hastening the implosion of the Habsburg Monarchy. Further damage was caused in April 1918 when the French Prime Minister Georges Clemenceau leaked and then published what became known as the 'Sixtus Letter'. In March 1917, only a few months after his accession to the throne, Emperor Karl had sounded out the possibility of a separate peace between the Allies and Austria-Hungary. Using his brother-in-law, Prince Sixtus of Bourbon-Parma (an officer in the Belgian army), as an intermediary, Karl wrote a letter to the French premier agreeing to a wide range of concessions, including the restitution to France of Alsace-Lorraine, to which Germany had helped herself as a spoil of the Franco-Prussian war. (Lorraine had once been the patrimony of Karl's great-great-great-great-grandfather Franz – husband of Maria Theresia and Holy Roman Emperor – but this ancestor had swapped it for Tuscany in 1735.) When the letter was made public, Foreign Minister Czernin made profuse denials, but nobody

PRESIDENT WILSON'S FOURTEEN POINTS, 8 JANUARY 1918

The program of the world's peace, therefore, is our program; and that program, the only possible program, as we see it, is this:

I. Open covenants of peace, openly arrived at, after which there shall be no private international understandings of any kind but diplomacy shall proceed always frankly and in the public view.

II. Absolute freedom of navigation upon the seas, outside territorial waters, alike in peace and in war, except as the seas may be closed in whole or in part by international action for the enforcement of international covenants.

III. The removal, so far as possible, of all economic barriers and the establishment of an equality of trade conditions among all the nations consenting to the peace and associating themselves for its maintenance.

IV. Adequate guarantees given and taken that national armaments will be reduced to the lowest point consistent with domestic safety.

V. A free, open-minded, and absolutely impartial adjustment of all colonial claims, based upon a strict observance of the principle that in determining all such questions of sovereignty the interests of the populations concerned must have equal weight with the equitable claims of the government whose title is to be determined.

VI. The evacuation of all Russian territory and such a settlement of all questions affecting Russia as will secure the best and freest cooperation of the other nations of the world in obtaining for her an unhampered and unembarrassed opportunity for the independent determination of her own political development and national policy and assure her of a sincere welcome into the society of free nations under institutions of her own choosing; and, more than a welcome, assistance also of every kind that she may need and may herself desire. The treatment accorded Russia by her sister nations in the months to come will be the acid test of their good will, of their comprehension of her needs as distinguished from their own interests, and of their intelligent and unselfish sympathy.

VII. Belgium, the whole world will agree, must be evacuated and restored, without any attempt to limit the sovereignty which she enjoys in common with all other free nations. No other single act will serve as this will serve to restore confidence among the nations in the laws which they have themselves set and determined for the government of their relations with one another. Without this healing act the whole structure and validity of international law is forever impaired.

VIII. All French territory should be freed and the invaded portions restored, and the wrong done to France by Prussia in 1871 in the matter of Alsace-Lorraine, which has unsettled the peace of the world for nearly fifty years, should be righted, in order that peace may once more be made secure in the interest of all.

IX. A readjustment of the frontiers of Italy should be effected along clearly recognizable lines of nationality.

X. The peoples of Austria-Hungary, whose place among the nations we wish to see safeguarded and assured, should be accorded the freest opportunity to autonomous development.

XI. Rumania, Serbia, and Montenegro should be evacuated; occupied territories restored; Serbia accorded free and secure access to the sea; and the relations of the several Balkan states to one another determined by friendly counsel along historically established lines of allegiance and nationality; and international guarantees of the political and economic independence and territorial integrity of the several Balkan states should be entered into.

XII. The Turkish portion of the present Ottoman Empire should be assured a secure sovereignty, but the other nationalities which are now under Turkish rule should be assured an undoubted security of life and an absolutely unmolested opportunity of autonomous development, and the Dardanelles should be permanently opened as a free passage to the ships and commerce of all nations under international guarantees.

XIII. An independent Polish state should be erected which should include the territories inhabited by indisputably Polish populations, which should be assured a free and secure access to the sea, and whose political and economic independence and territorial integrity should be guaranteed by international covenant.

XIV. A general association of nations must be formed under specific covenants for the purpose of affording mutual guarantees of political independence and territorial integrity to great and small states alike.

was fooled. Furious German nationalists forced Karl to go, tail between his legs, to meet with the Kaiser in Belgium, where he submitted to his more powerful ally, making the Monarchy practically a puppet of Imperial Germany for the remainder of the War. Czernin resigned.

Not only were the food queues in cities getting longer, troops at the front now lacked rations, munitions and uniforms. And yet there was no resolution to the military stalemate. Ludendorff's great offensive, a final attempt to break through on the Western Front, failed, as did Austria-Hungary's attack on Italy in June. When the Bulgarian front cracked in September, even the Germans had had enough. The Central Powers sued for an armistice. In a hopeless, last-ditch attempt to save his empire, or at least some of it, Karl issued a manifesto on 16 October proclaiming the Austrian half of the Monarchy to be a federal state with complete autonomy for the nationalities. But nobody was listening.

The territory of the Habsburg Monarchy ended up divided between seven sovereign states. Transylvania and the Bukovina became part of Romania; Upper Hungary (largely Slovak-speaking) and Carpathian Ruthenia joined with Bohemia, Moravia and Silesia to form Czechoslovakia; the Kingdom of Croatia-Slavonia, together with Bosnia and Herzegovina, Carniola and most of Dalmatia joined Serbia and Montenegro to form Yugoslavia; South Tyrol, Trieste, Istria, and a variety of other Adriatic possessions were joined to Italy; and Galicia went to the reconstituted Polish Republic. This left Austria and Hungary.

The Poles had already gone their own way, a Czech national committee was virtually in charge of Bohemia, a 'National Council of Serbs, Croats and Slovenes' had established itself in Zagreb on 6 October, and even the German deputies of the Reichsrat met to discuss their possible future. Hungary, which was untouched by the manifesto, started to prepare for an independent existence.

THE ANSCHLUSS MOVEMENT

The twin motors of the 1848 revolutions were nationalism and liberalism. The Parliament that convened at Frankfurt from May 1848 to May 1849, and which represented all the states of the German Confederation, harnessed both these forces to proclaim a German Empire based on the principles of parliamentary democracy. This pan-German scheme (known as the 'big German' solution) disintegrated into the rubble of the revolution, after which Prussia, Bismarck in particular, worked successfully to exclude the Habsburg German possessions from the unification process which resulted in the creation of the German Empire in 1871 (the 'small German' solution).

In the closing decades of the 19th century, only a minority of German nationalists in Austria advocated union with Germany, or Anschluss. These were led by the fiery Georg von Schönerer, a former liberal turned rabid nationalist who attacked the multinational Habsburg state at every opportunity, and who influenced the political development of Adolf Hitler and the National Socialist Party. Socialism in Austria also preserved the 1848 spirit for a while, but the Social Democratic Party was founded and led by moderate figures who aimed at reform within the empire rather than its destruction. The vast majority of Germans in the Monarchy harboured no thoughts of Anschluss.

When the Habsburg Empire disintegrated at the end of the War, it was no surprise that the Anschluss movement, now spearheaded by the Social Democrats, experienced a rapid growth in adherents amongst German-Austrians. But support for Anschluss was by no means universal. The Paris Peace Conference, which prohibited the union of Germany and Austria, dealt a serious blow to the movement, leadership of which gradually passed into the hands of the bourgeois Pan-German Party. Another wave of Anschluss enthusiasm briefly accompanied the customs union plan of 1931, after which the movement became the preserve of the Austrian National Socialists and government policy in Vienna was set firmly on independence.

With the Monarchy in freefall, Renner clung to his belief that it had a future, still arguing that the multinational state was a superior form of political organisation than the nation-state. It is unsurprising therefore, given this unswerving loyalty to the Empire, that Renner's name kept on cropping up in relation to a ministerial post, even that of Minister President. Indeed, the Emperor offered Renner the post in October, but the Social Democrats again rejected his candidature, asserting that they did not want to be in charge of a sinking ship. Meanwhile, the entry of the Social Democrats in Germany into Max von Baden's government caused a great upsurge of support for Anschluss – political union with Germany – amongst their German-Austrian colleagues.

On 21 October the German deputies of the Reichsrat met in Vienna and this group constituted itself as the Provisional National Assembly for German-Austria. On 11 November, Emperor Karl issued a proclamation in which he professed love for all his peoples and promised he would not stand in the way of their future development. He recognised in advance the form of government that 'German-Austria' would decide on (the German crownlands were all that was left of Austria) and renounced any further participation in state affairs. This last clause – Renner supposedly had a hand in its formulation – was something of a fudge; it did not strictly amount to an abdication, and left the door open for a possible return to the throne. As Chancellor some months later, Renner unsuccessfully attempted to make Karl sign an official abdication.

Meanwhile, the transition was moving fast and Renner was at the centre of events. Hungary and Bohemia had blocked all exports to Austria, which meant that alternative food sources were urgently needed to feed the starving population. On 23 October Renner made an unsuccessful trip to Berlin as part of a delegation seeking flour and cereals. Once back in Vienna, he was given the task of devising a statute for the new state, which he referred to as *Südostdeutschland* (South-Eastern Germany). Like the majority of his compatriots, Renner did not believe that the small German-Austrian state, severed from its vast hinterland, was a viable prospect. Given the hostility of the Czechoslovak, Yugoslav and Hungarian states towards Vienna, a Danube Federation of the former territories of the Monarchy looked highly unlikely, leaving Anschluss as the only option for rump Austria.

At the second sitting of the Provisional National Assembly in Vienna on 30 October 1918, Renner presented the House with a provisional constitution. He called on workers, farmers and the middle classes to unite and cooperate in the new state. At their recent conference the Social Democrats had agreed to work together with the bourgeois parties in an attempt to effect as smooth a transition as possible and prevent the sort of revolution that had erupted in Germany. Even Otto Bauer attempted to quell the revolutionary spirit. So a provisional government was formed from all the parties, and the accommodating but wily Renner became *de facto* head of government, largely – it now seems – as a result of his own scheming. He attributed far more authority to his administrative post than it officially carried, and nobody chose to contradict him.[7] Victor Adler, although ill with a serious heart condition at the time, was put in charge of foreign affairs. Renner also designed a coat of arms for the new state, and would later compose the words of a national anthem (which, however, never really caught on).

On 12 November the German-Austrian Republic was proclaimed, with Renner as self-appointed State Chancellor. Tragically, Adler had died the day before; Bauer took over his portfolio as Foreign Minister. German-Austria was declared to be a constituent part of the German Republic. In his speech to mark this historic event, Renner affirmed his commitment to Anschluss, emphasising the historical, cultural and ethnic ties between the Germans of Austria and their brothers in Germany. He also talked about a League of Nations for Europe, to protect the Continent from the imperialist designs of the Anglo-Saxon bourgeoisie. That same day there was an attempted Bolshevik putsch in Vienna which failed miserably. The zeal of Austrian Social Democracy for party unity had paid off. Unlike in Germany, where the socialists had split in 1917, communism was unable to garner much support in Austria. Revolutionary activity was thus isolated and insignificant.

Karl Renner, now 47 years old, had reached the apex of political power in his homeland. If his assumption of the reins of government had been unorthodox, it must be remembered that these were extraordinary times. What is more, Renner's slightly authoritarian mode of political manoeuvring, which would again be in evidence in 1945, only ever had as its aim the strengthening of the democratic system. A challenging 18 months now lay ahead of the new Chancellor. His first task was to stabilise the German-Austrian state internally, and then to seek as favourable a settlement as possible with the Allied Powers at the forthcoming Peace Conference.

Renner at the Peace Conference in summer 1919. As representatives of an Enemy Power, the Austrian delegation was kept under strict supervision.

II
The Paris Peace Conference

4
Prelude to the Treaty

The circumstances into which the First Republic of Austria was born were inauspicious for the future of the state. Essentially, rump Austria was a negative construction: it was what was left (as Clemenceau famously said in St Germain) once the other peoples of the western half of the Monarchy had carved off territories for their own states. No consideration was given to the economic consequences of isolation for German-Austria, nor to the wishes of the many ethnic Germans who were caught in foreign states. This was particularly true of Czechoslovakia. Without waiting for the deliberations of the Peace Conference, Czech troops occupied the Sudeten areas of Bohemia and Moravia, thus denying three million ethnic Germans a say in where the post-war borders should be drawn. On 22 November 1918 the Provisional National Assembly in Vienna had passed a law defining the boundaries of the German-Austrian state. On the insistence of the Pan-German deputies, German-Austria laid claim to the German enclaves of Brünn, Iglau and Olmütz (Czech: Brno, Jihlava and Olomouc), but the government in Vienna was powerless to enforce the declaration.

The situation on Austria's other borders was no less problematical. As part of the 1915 Treaty of London the Entente Powers had promised Italy the South Tyrol. After the crushing Italian victory at Vittorio Veneto in late October 1918, which precipitated the collapse of the Monarchy, Austria-Hungary was pushed back far beyond its pre-1914 borders, and Italian troops duly occupied the whole of the Tyrol, including Innsbruck. In the south-east there were skirmishes with units from the new Kingdom of Serbs, Croats and Slovenes (Yugoslavia), which laid claim to parts of Carinthia. To the east, on the other hand, lay a narrow strip of territory that was an integral part of Hungary, but which was solidly German by population, and thus became a target of Austrian revisionism.

Prior to the outbreak of the First World War, Italy was part of the Triple Alliance with Germany and Austria-Hungary. The Entente Powers lured Italy away from this association with the promise of generous spoils after the War, including the South Tyrol, Trieste and northern Dalmatia. The Treaty of London was signed on 26 April 1915, and Italy duly declared war on Austria-Hungary a month later (it did not actually declare war on Germany until August 1916). President Wilson did not consider himself bound by the treaty as the United States had not been party to it, so he disputed many of the Italian claims in Paris. Disagreements over the Italian borders clogged up the workings of the Conference in 1919.

As the head of a government that had to bridge the political divide, Karl Renner had little time to devote to his own party – Otto Bauer was now the ideological leader of the Social Democrats. Neither did he have much room for his private life, given the turmoil and uncertainty all around him. Nonetheless, he was able to draw on the security he felt from his immediate family which, allied to a stable personality, enabled him to weather the storms of the immediate post-war months. The blockade on exports imposed by Austria's neighbours did not just affect food supplies, but fuel as well. Bohemia had been the chief coal producer of the Monarchy, and now many Viennese industries were forced to stop production for a lack of fuel. Meanwhile, there was tension within German-Austria itself, as the individual provinces – the old crownlands – were keeping food for themselves rather than releasing it to the starving capital. In this early hostility between Vienna and the provinces we can see the beginnings of the conflict between Social Democratic centralism and Christian Social federalism which would weaken the cohesion of the First Republic.

> 'Everybody looks very pinched and yellow: no fats for four years.'
> **HAROLD NICOLSON'S FIRST IMPRESSION OF POST-WAR VIENNA**[1]

The situation in Vienna was so acute that in early 1919 the meat supply had been exhausted. There was a shortage of potatoes and milk for the children and the sick, while the poorest people in the capital were wearing wooden shoes and clothes made of paper. It was in these conditions that the Republic's first elections were held in February 1919, with women having been given the vote for the first time. The Social Democrats emerged as the largest party with 72 seats, the Christian Socials were a close second with 69, while the Pan-Germans won 26 seats in the new Constituent Assembly. With only a relative rather than overall majority, the Social Democrats had to renew the pre-election coalition. This strengthened Renner's hand, as he was the man for compromise, even though he was fairly isolated in his own party. In addition to the Chancellorship he took the internal affairs and education portfolios. Otto Bauer, the leading pro-Anschluss figure in Austria, remained Foreign Minister, and Julius Deutsch became Army Minister.

The first food aid arrived from Italy in January 1919, while two months later the Allies granted Austria a credit of $30 million to purchase basic foodstuffs. But this only bought a short amount of time, and did nothing to tackle the structural problems of the Austrian economy. In May 1919, it was reported that children in Vienna were scraping by on a diet of 800 calories per day, rather than the necessary 1,500–2,000.[2] Substantial volumes of supplies were, however, being smuggled from Hungary and Czechoslovakia, fuelling a roaring black-market trade for those who could afford the exorbitant prices. Moreover, the situation elsewhere in Austria was nowhere near as grim. A British officer reported in April 1919 that the food supply in Innsbruck was not short and prices were reasonable.[3] But, as we have already noted, the clerical, conservative provinces were hostile towards 'Red Vienna' – which was home to around a third of the country's population – and highly reluctant to supply the capital with provisions. This feeling of being isolated and under siege in its Viennese fortress fed the appetite amongst Social Democrats for union with Germany, where since the November 1918 revolution their fellow socialists were by far the strongest party.

In the aftermath of the War and the break-up of the Habsburg Empire, the Social Democrats in Austria were the driving force behind the Anschluss movement. The Pan-German party, traditionally the home of German nationalism, was now more reticent in its backing for union with a socialist Germany. The Christian Socials were, on the whole, pretty lukewarm in their attitude towards Anschluss. Like the Pan-Germans, they were not encouraged by the political developments in Germany, but other reasons also forged an attitude which, in some quarters, went beyond scepticism as far as outright hostility. A significant proportion of the Party harboured strong monarchist sympathies; for these Anschluss was to be rejected because of its incompatibility with a restoration of the House of Habsburg. As a clerical conservative party, moreover, the Christian Socials feared that Austria's Catholic identity would be swamped by a Prussian-dominated (and thus Protestant) Reich. The Christian Social alternative to Anschluss was a Danube federation, essentially a reconstituted superstate in Central Europe, consisting of those successor states who wished to join, and preferably under the sceptre of the Habsburgs.

With Bauer as Foreign Minister, it might have been expected that Austria would push hard for an early implementation of Anschluss. In October 1918, he wrote a series of articles for the socialist press laying down the theoretical foundation for Anschluss, and insisting on the impossibility of a separate existence for German-Austria.[4] And over the next nine months he consistently followed a policy which aimed at the realisation of this goal. However, unlike his impulsive and fiercely pro-union ambassador in Berlin, Ludo Hartmann, Bauer was tactical in his approach to the Anschluss question. This was in part occasioned by the attitude of the Germans themselves, who maintained a cautious Anschluss policy from the armistice until the signing of the Treaty of Versailles. From a German perspective, union with Austria was only one of a number of issues thrown up by the outcome of the War, and by no means the most important. There were the questions of the territories on its eastern and western borders, and Germany had no wish to prejudice the fate of these at the Peace Conference by improvident and premature moves towards the implementation of Anschluss. Austria, too, might hope that a more discreet Anschluss policy could result in a more favourable outcome in Paris.

The French and Czechosolvaks were both hostile to Anschluss: the French saw no reason why Germany should be rewarded with a territorial gain after defeat in a war in which it had wrought much havoc; the Czechoslovaks, meanwhile, feared being surrounded on three sides by an enemy state that would inevitably seek to exploit the sizeable German minority in western Czechoslovakia. Although the French were always categorical in their opposition to a German-Austrian union, the Americans and British were far more equivocal in their attitude, at least initially. Indeed, the US Secretary of State Robert Lansing proposed in September 1918 that the German part of Austria should become part of the German federal state.[5] Meanwhile, the Political Intelligence Department of the British Foreign Office warned in December 1918 that one could not prevent the Austrians from feeling German; to do so might stimulate German nationalism. In any case, this memorandum continued, Anschluss might even benefit Britain, as Austria would help restore the balance between the Catholic South and Protestant North, and check Prussian domination of Germany.[6] A substantial proportion of Italian public opinion, meanwhile, favoured Anschluss over a Danube federation. For Italy, the Habsburg Empire rather than Germany had been the chief enemy. In the French-sponsored scheme to organise the small states of Central Europe into a political association, Italy saw nothing less than the re-establishment of a German- and Magyar-dominated Monarchy.

Eventually, the three other Powers came round to the French point of view; in April 1919, during discussions of the Versailles Treaty, the Council of Four – Wilson, Clemenceau, Lloyd George and Orlando – agreed that Germany must be obliged to recognise the independence of Austria. Wilson had been uneasy about such a flagrant violation of the principle of self-determination, but when Lloyd George proposed a compromise – that the ban on Anschluss might be lifted in future if it met with the approval of the League of Nations – this seemed to satisfy the American President.

Given the known hostility in France to Anschluss, therefore, Bauer paid lip-service to the idea of a Danube federation, and also acted to restrain the Austrian ambassador to Germany in his energetic campaign for union. Nonetheless, when the German Parliament in Weimar – in a show of support that went beyond anything the actual German government had dared to express – passed a resolution on 21 February 1919 in favour of Anschluss, Bauer decided to visit Berlin for discussions. The week-long negotiations resulted in a protocol signed on 2 March which laid the groundwork for Austria's entry into a federal Germany as a separate member state. The details of the treaty were not made public, and both sides agreed that nothing should be implemented until the peace treaties had been signed.

The instructions drafted for the Austrian delegation to Paris were neither signed nor dated, but it is likely that Bauer drew them up himself sometime in April or early May 1919. The guidelines stipulated that the Austrians themselves should not initiate discussion of the Anschluss question, but debate the issue only if the Allies raised it or presented terms which would make union impossible. If the delegation was forced to defend its corner, it was advised to stress the economic difficulties that an independent Austria faced. The delegates should further point out that the idea of a Danube federation was doomed by opposition from the Poles, Romanians and probably the South Slavs as well. At all events, Anschluss should only be considered once the territorial deliberations and the most important economic questions were already settled.

The delegation was warned that it should not be too

assertive in its approach to the Peace Conference; Austria was, after all, a weak state. So while it must insist on the right of national self-determination – a key theme of the Conference – it ought not to make its demands too forcefully. With regard to specific territorial issues, the instructions directed the delegation to strive for 'full self-determination' rather than mere autonomy for the German regions of Czechoslovakia, and push for the retention of the South Tyrol (which Italy claimed by virtue of the Treaty of London) while offering that the region be neutralised militarily. The guidelines also contained advice for negotiating the two other contested borders – with Hungary in the west and Yugoslavia in the south-east.[7]

It is possible that these instructions were formulated with the expectation that the peace delegation would be headed by Franz Klein, a minister under Bauer in the Austrian Foreign Office and a strong supporter of Anschluss. From November onwards he had been in charge of the preparations for the Conference, but the French were opposed to his leading the Austrian mission, and so Klein ended up going to Paris as an ordinary member of the team. In his history of the First Republic, Renner suggests that he was chosen as head of the Austrian delegation because he had the most thorough understanding of the national problem and was also well acquainted with leading politicians from the other nationalities. In truth Renner was again the compromise candidate – he was actually the fifth choice as delegation leader – and definitely acceptable to the Entente Powers who still saw him as an old Austrian patriot, in spite of the fact that he had recently embraced the cause of Anschluss.

The Peace Conference had opened in Paris on 18 January 1919, and had first focused on drafting a covenant for the new League of Nations, after which attention was turned to the Treaty with Germany. On 1 May an invitation was sent to Vienna, asking the Austrians to schedule their arrival in the French capital for the middle of that month. The Austrian delegation totalled 60 members, which included representatives from the other two main political parties, as well as around 30 experts, 8 journalists and 15 staff. As the delegation made the necessary preparations for their departure, the German peace terms were published (7 May). The perceived harshness of these stunned the Austrians, and held out little hope for their own cause. The principle of national self-determination seemed to have been ignored in the Germans' case; more specifically, the terms included an obligation on Germany's part to respect the independence of Austria, in other words putting a prohibition on Anschluss. The Austrian *Neue Freie Presse* talked of the responsibility the Conference Powers would have to bear towards the Austrian state if they forced on it an independence it did not want.[8] The Christian Social *Reichspost* was less concerned about the Anschluss ban – criticising as it did the 'rushed' and 'clumsy' policy of both Germany and Austria in this respect – and more about the 'horrific' fate of the Germans in the Czechoslovak state, who could have little to hope for now from the Austrian treaty.[9]

When the Austrian delegates left for France on 12 May, therefore, they knew that a tough time awaited them. The crowds in Vienna urged Renner to bring them back a good peace. In reply he said: *We are going into the unknown; we have no idea what the results will be.* He promised to obtain all that was humanly possible, but he reminded the Austrians that they had lost the War and cautioned them to be realistic in their expectations.[10] Franz Klein (who documented the Peace Conference in letters written to his lover back in Vienna, and whose gloomy demeanour throughout the summer of 1919 was in sharp contrast to Renner's optimism) noted that as the delegation approached Paris they could sense an increasing hostility from the French population.[11]

Renner made an immediate impact upon arrival in the French capital. On 16 May *The Times* reported that the Austrian delegation gave the impression of being anything but enemies. The paper contrasted the 'haggard' leader of the German delegation, the Foreign Minister Ulrich von Brockdorff-Rantzau, with the 'beaming' Renner, who apologised in broken French for his poor command of the language, and then continued his greetings in German.[13] The French papers also praised Renner's moderate tone, remarking how different his approach was from that of the Germans.[14]

'This is the first time I have come amongst you. I do so with great satisfaction. I hope I shall have equal reason to be satisfied when I leave you.'
RENNER ON HIS ARRIVAL IN PARIS, MAY 1919[12]

Austria's representatives at the Peace Conference were housed in ten villas in the Rue de Médicis, which backed onto a park. Renner took the Villa Reinach which provided him with a large study and a library. *The Times* correspondent admitted a certain 'envy' for the delegates 'who will spend the next few weeks lodged on the edge of a terrace overlooking the valley of the Seine, with the summer foliage of the park at their backs'.[15] But the idyllic location was undermined by the conditions of the Austrians' sojourn in Paris. The delegation, it must be remembered, was representing an enemy power and they were treated as such. Franz Klein likened the delegates to prisoners who were just better fed and enjoyed more fresh air than convicts.[16] They were isolated from the outside world, always under guard, and given permission to move within an area of three streets only, as well as in a section of the park closed off by barbed wire. After several weeks, the delegation was then allowed to make excursions on Sundays in military vehicles. Allied officers were prohibited from shaking hands with the Austrians. There was also to be no face-to-face negotiation of the Peace Treaty; any comments or objections the Austrian delegation might have would have to take the form of written notes.

Nevertheless, compared with their shattered and impoverished country, Paris must have seemed like Paradise to the Austrians, especially as far as the food was concerned. With one of his letters Klein attached a cutting from a French newspaper reporting on the dinner the Austrians had enjoyed on their first evening: *potage cressonnière* (cream of watercress and potato soup), *tête de veau vinaigrette* (calf's head with vinaigrette dressing), *asperges mousseline* (asparagus mousse), *viande froide* (cold meats), *dessert*.[17] Klein dismissed, however, the satirical reports appearing in the press back in Vienna, which claimed the delegates were living it up in Paris; he insisted that everybody's behaviour was highly respectable. Mindful of the plight of their countrymen, the delegation soon took the decision to pay for wine and snacks out of their own purses, rather than have the Austrian state cover all expenses.

For someone who loved to eat, and in generous quantities, Renner found it very hard to turn down the plentiful offerings that came his way. On 21 June he wrote that he had bloated terribly in the first fortnight and could notice his clothes getting tighter. As there were no scales, however, he could not tell whether he was putting on weight. Renner's secretary was in no doubt. She wrote back to his wife, Luise, 'I must say that I was almost horrified when I saw the Herr Dr. The food is in such abundance that he's becoming incredibly large … almost every day roast meat appears twice on the menu. I've got Prof Laun to monitor him … Unfortunately he's not firm enough.' [18]

Renner immediately took command of the delegation, splitting it into two groups and organising daily meetings. His daily routine in Paris seldom varied. He would wake early at half-past five and then get up very slowly and drink several cups of coffee. Between seven and eight he would take a walk in the park behind his villa. Then he would wash and get dressed, and at half-past eight eat the morning rolls prepared for him by his secretary (who no doubt took care in limiting the dimensions of his breakfast). Between nine and ten Renner read the French newspapers on his sofa, followed by two hours of office work – what he called 'bureau'. Official meetings and press conferences took place between twelve and half-past, after which there was an hour for lunch, and then coffee and cigars in the lounge. At two Renner would take a little walk and then half-an-hour's nap. More office work followed between three and seven, which generally rounded off the working day. The delegation would dine at seven, take an hour's walk together in the park, and then spend the rest of the evening playing cards or holding the occasional meeting. Bed was usually at half-past midnight. [19]

One reason why this routine became so ingrained was that the Austrians were practically ignored when they arrived in Paris. They had evidently been called to St Germain prematurely, as the Allies were still some way from agreeing the details of the draft treaty. On 24 May Renner wrote to Clemenceau wishing to know why the peace terms had not yet been handed over. Klein thought that Renner had missed an opportunity to demand some sort of personal contact with the French Premier.[20] In fact, Klein was critical of Renner throughout his stay in Paris. Although he initially wrote that he got on well with the Chancellor and found him a more amicable personality than Otto Bauer, Klein soon felt that Renner was out of his depth and floundering. On 30 May he wrote that his leadership of the country was slipping through his fingers, and that Bauer, with his superior intellect, would have been a better choice to head the delegation after all.[21] Klein, no doubt, still felt quite bitter that Renner had landed the top job in Paris instead of him; this rancour was exacerbated by the Chancellor's obstinacy. Once Renner had something in his head, Klein said, no persuasion from the rest of the delegation could make him change his mind.[22]

Still the Austrian representatives were made to wait. The Council of Four continued to be preoccupied with details pertaining to the German treaty, while a lot of time was also taken up haggling over Italian territorial claims. The Austrian treaty was low on the list of the Council's priorities.[23] Klein now admitted that some of the 'provincial' members were just enjoying themselves rather than making a useful contribution to the delegation's work. He also revealed that there was talk of the Austrians leaving Paris altogether, either some or all of them.[24] The mood in the camp – or at least in part of it – was not improved when the delegation learned that their state was to be called Austria rather than German-Austria. Klein thundered against this 'contemptuous' disregard for national self-determination: 'Do we have to hide the fact that we're German?' He also noted rather acidly that this 'shocking' attempt to 'denationalize' the Austrians merely drew a sigh from the Chancellor.[25]

For a fortnight the Austrian delegation faced a tense wait

in their St Germain confinement. Finally, official notification arrived from the Council of Four that the terms of the Treaty would be presented on 2 June. Renner and his fellow delegates knew well that the document would not make pretty reading; the draft Treaty of Versailles had shown that the Allies were prepared to get tough with the Enemy Powers. More specifically, details from the German treaty meant that the Austrians already knew what to expect regarding the question of Anschluss. Renner had made the best possible impact on his arrival in Paris. It remained to be seen whether this favourable impression might assist Austria's cause with the Entente Powers.

5

The Treaty of St Germain

On 2 June 1919 the Austrian delegation was driven to the Renaissance castle in St Germain-en-Laye to come face-to-face with the Council representatives and their associates. The Austrians were ushered in through the back entrance, and then made to hang around for an hour in the waiting room while the Allied delegates assembled. These had been called for 11.45 a.m., but Lloyd George did not arrive until 12.05 p.m. Wilson, meanwhile, had car trouble; he was 15 minutes late, too.[1]

When the Austrians were finally admitted to the hall at 12.30 p.m., there could be no mistaking that they were present as an Enemy Power. Representatives of the Allied Powers and their associates sat in a large horseshoe, at the open end of which stood a table for the leading figures of the Austrian delegation. Renner was solemnly handed the peace terms which were in English, French and Italian but not German.[2] Clemenceau explained that there could be no verbal discussion of these terms; any observations the Austrian delegation might wish to make would have to be submitted in writing within 15 days. The Supreme Council would then inform the Austrians of the deadline by which they would have to formulate their definitive reply to the Treaty as a whole. The gravitas of the ceremony was undercut when Clemenceau's translator made an error, addressing Renner and his colleagues as the 'German-Austrian' delegation, whereas the French Premier, wary of giving the slightest encouragement to the Anschluss movement, had been very careful in referring only to the 'Austrian' Republic. He immediately corrected his translator who was interrupted again when a photographer, straining to reach a good vantage point, put his foot through a glass case and sent it crashing to the floor.[3]

To Clemenceau's embarrassment the peace terms handed to Renner were incomplete. What the Austrians received that day was only the first part of the Treaty, as the Entente Powers were still squabbling over matters such as the borders with Italy and Yugoslavia. Moreover, much of the text had been simply lifted from the draft German treaty. Thus the delegation was surprised to learn that Austria – now a landlocked country – was forbidden to have submarines.[4] Similar bewilderment must have greeted the requirement for Austria to renounce all claims to, and titles in, Morocco, Egypt, China and Siam (Thailand).

The terms did not mention Anschluss directly, but stipulated that the existing frontier between Austria and Bavaria was to be maintained. The border with Czechoslovakia was to follow the former administrative boundaries between Lower Austria on the one hand, and Bohemia and Moravia on the other, except for some very minor alterations along ethnic lines in favour of the Czechs. To the east, the border between Austria and Hungary was to remain that of the 1867 settlement, while in the south the draft Treaty confirmed the loss of the southern part of the Tyrol to Italy, although the exact frontier had not yet been agreed on. There was even stronger disagreement over the Austro-Yugoslav border, particularly with regard to the Klagenfurt basin; apparently Clemenceau had to tear that section out of the peace terms just prior to handing them over to Renner.[5]

The preamble to the Treaty noted Austria-Hungary's responsibility in starting the conflict by its declaration of war against Serbia, but also that Austria-Hungary no longer existed as a political entity. The Treaty also included: an outline of the League of Nations, detailing its structure, membership, aims and procedure; a political section dealing with the protection of minorities, and also obliging Austria to recognise the new map of Europe; articles relating to prisoners of war; a provision for possible war crimes trials; and a number of economic clauses, one of which sanctioned the confiscation of property held by Austrians within other successor states to the Monarchy. Reparations clauses and financial clauses were classified as 'reserved', to be dealt with later. One major difference from the German treaty was the decision to treat the last Habsburg Emperor more favourably than the Kaiser. Whereas the Allies planned to put Wilhelm II on trial 'for a supreme offence against international morality and the sanctity of treaties' (Article 227 of the Treaty of Versailles), they recognised that not only had Karl succeeded to the throne half-way through the War, he had also made a number of clumsy attempts to exit it as quickly as possible. The sins of Franz Joseph were not to be visited on his great-nephew.

Unlike his German counterpart, Renner addressed the representatives of the Allied Powers and their associates in French, which impressed the home delegation. Klein wrote that Renner had ignored advice to use German for his speech, just another example of the Chancellor's stubbornness.[6] After all, he was not fluent in the language, but had prepared his speech thoroughly with the help of an elderly French lady employed in the Austrian Foreign Office who ensured that each word was pronounced correctly.[7] Renner told the assembly that German-Austria had been waiting nervously for this fateful day to arrive; the uncertainty over the peace terms had created great tension in his country. The Austro-Hungarian Monarchy was dead, he asserted, and, although he agreed with Clemenceau that the change in government and political system could not completely absolve German-Austria of its share of war guilt, nonetheless this burden should not be shouldered by Austria alone. Renner argued that German-Austria was a brand new entity – not a continuation of the Empire – and, having come into existence only after the cessation of hostilities, it had not been at war with any other state. He observed how other successor states to the Monarchy were being treated quite differently from Austria at the Peace Conference, and hoped that this contradiction would be rectified.

Renner appealed to the representatives of the Entente before him and, as Klein conceded, imbued his words with a great deal of feeling.[8] *We are before you as one of the parts of the vanquished and fallen Empire*, he said. *Ready to assume our proportion of the liabilities grown out of these our relations to the Allied Powers, we are well aware that our fate is resting in your hands.* He urged the victors not to deny German-Austria the right to national self-determination that had been cited as a principal war aim, and which was currently enjoyed by its neighbours. He explained that the fragmentation of the Monarchy as an economic unit had caused the people of German-Austria to suffer far more than they had in wartime; only through generous relief action by the Allies had his compatriots escaped starvation. They had borne this hardship, Renner said, *with discipline, patient endurance and good judgement.* He cited the bloodless revolution from monarchy to republic and the abstention from any military action against Austria's neighbours – in spite of the fact that they occupied two-fifths of its territory. Renner concluded by hoping that the Entente would listen to German-Austria as they had listened to its neighbours, and he prayed that the Allies would finally come to a decision which would ensure the survival of his country.[9] He did not explicitly demand union with Germany as a remedy for Austria's ills, a tactic which met with criticism from German quarters; it was felt that Renner's approach was far too conciliatory towards the Allies.[11]

> 'We trust that the world's common sense ... will not permit our economic ruin.'
> RENNER BEFORE THE ALLIES, 2 JUNE 1919[10]

When the delegation returned to their quarters they were dismayed. Renner's secretary wrote to Luise: 'We're all very depressed. The peace is more severe than ... the German peace.'[12] The treaty confirmed the *status quo* in Central Europe: more than four million Germans of the old Monarchy were to be placed under foreign sovereignty. The terms were even worse than had been anticipated. Even the French papers, which had shown admiration for Renner's demeanour, thought them excessively harsh.[13] Renner's immediate reaction at a press conference was that the peace terms were not only unjust; they left Austria an unviable state. Back in Vienna, an emergency cabinet meeting was summoned, at which Bauer said very little and just sat there moodily.[14] He immediately contacted the German Foreign Office to seek diplomatic assistance over the Sudeten question, but the reply from Berlin was that such a move was inopportune given the present circumstances.[15]

Bauer was not only fuming at the Treaty itself, but also at the reserve Renner had shown in pushing the Anschluss issue with the Allies. It will be recalled that Bauer's own guidelines for the Austrian delegation had advised a cautious approach to the Anschluss question in Paris, but as far as the Foreign Minister was concerned, Renner's approach had been too circumspect. Intended to win more favourable terms for Austria, the Chancellor's strategy had clearly failed. Bauer left with President Karl Seitz and Vice-Chancellor Jodok Fink of the Christian Social Party to meet Renner at Feldkirch on the Swiss-Austrian border. There they would discuss the peace terms and attempt to devise a plan for the way ahead.

Not surprisingly, the Austrian public was indignant when the peace terms became known. Particular vitriol was reserved for the Minor Powers, whose influence – it was widely believed – had turned what might have otherwise been a favourable treaty against Austria. One wisecrack suggested that the Czechoslovak President Masaryk was Wilson's brother-in-law, while elsewhere Poland, Czechoslovakia, Romania and Yugoslavia were referred to as the 'four sisters' bent on Austria's destruction. The press queued up to denounce the injustice of the Treaty. One paper called it 'a crime against mankind and all her high and noble ideas', while another quipped that it had been sent to the wrong address. The chief targets of their criticism were the territorial and economic clauses of the terms. The idea that Klagenfurt, a town of around 25,000 Germans and 500 Slovenes – and which Yugoslav forces occupied on 6 June – might be lost without a plebiscite signalled a betrayal of the Wilsonian principle of national self-determination. Meanwhile, the article allowing the confiscation of German-Austrian property in the successor states was seen as a death-blow. The demand for Anschluss became ever louder.[16]

Renner announced to his compatriots that he would register a strong protest in Paris. The conservative Austrian daily, *Reichspost*, reported his promise that the delegation would *make it immediately clear to the leaders of the Entente that, if they compel German-Austria to conclude this treaty, they will be endangering their own triumph by loading a corpse onto the victory chariot.*[17] On 10 June Renner passed the delegation's initial reply, which Klein was horrified to see had been drafted without his input, to the Council.[18] The German-Austrian government was obliged, it began, to point out to the Allied Powers that the Treaty in its present form would rob the country 'of absolutely indispensable means for the maintenance of its economic and social order'. It emphasised that the peace terms deprived German-Austria of some of its richest and most fertile areas, while placing four out of ten million Germans under 'hostile foreign domination'. The state envisaged by the Treaty, which consisted of just the Alpine lands plus Vienna, could not survive. This rump Austria, it argued, would only be able to produce one-quarter of the food necessary to feed its population; the rest would have to be imported. The situation with regard to fuel was even more acute, it continued. Austria could only produce two million tons of coal annually, whereas its consumption was 14 million tons. It would, moreover, be impossible to cover these imports with exports as all export industries had been stripped from German-Austria. In short, Austria was threatened by economic collapse, the note warned, which could only have grave consequences for the whole of Central Europe.[19] Following on from this written response, the

Chancellor wrote a series of other notes with the object of trying to improve the peace terms. In July he also paid a visit to the President of the Entente's Economic Council pleading for food aid, without which, Renner argued, it would be impossible to maintain social order in Austria.

The tiny Alpine *Land* of Vorarlberg, on the very western tip of Austria, had already challenged the integrity of the new state. On the eve of the delegation's departure for Paris, it held a plebiscite on the issue of joining the Swiss Confederation as a new canton. The provincial assembly had rejected the National Assembly's decision on Anschluss. Vorarlberg's governor and later Austrian Chancellor, Otto Ender, argued that the *Land* did not belong to the Danube area; it was divided from the rest of Austria by mountains. He also asserted that, racially and linguistically, the Vorarlbergers were closer to the Swiss than to other German-speaking peoples.[20] Whatever the validity of Ender's arguments, the Vorarlbergers felt sufficiently strongly on the issue for 80.6 per cent of them to vote in favour of union with Switzerland. The Swiss themselves took a more cautious line, insisting that the matter could not proceed any further without the consent of the Allied Powers and the Austrian federal government. Although this independent move ultimately came to nothing, the case of Vorarlberg demonstrated that attachment to rump Austria was so weak and the sense of historic rights and provincial identity so great, that individual *Länder* had the confidence to defy the Republic and take unilateral action.

One of the many notes that the industrious Chancellor sent to the Entente was a plea to join the League of Nations. The delegation stated that the League had a 'special and unique significance' for German-Austria, given the history of the different peoples who had co-existed in the Danube lands. Without a permanent arbitral tribunal, the note argued, lasting peace in the region would be impossible. German-Austria registered its disappointment that it would have to undergo a period of probation before being admitted for membership. The country was committed to peace and respect for other nationalities, and deserved better treatment than the attitude of mistrust that currently prevailed. 'Of all the newly formed states,' the note continued, 'German-Austria is the only one which, from its very foundation, has left to the Peace Congress the settlement of all questions in dispute, and has without reserve confided her cause to the Powers for their decision.' This was in contrast to Czechoslovakia, Yugoslavia and Hungary, all of which had deployed military force to effect territorial changes which must prejudice the decisions of the Conference. If the questionable actions of these countries were to be rewarded by admission to the League, and German-Austria denied membership, then how could the Austrian population have faith in the League and favour peaceful resolution of conflict over settlement by force? As soon as it was a fully-fledged member of the League and 'enjoyed the benefits of a really just peace', German-Austria promised to become a bastion of the new world order and a beacon of peace. This note to the Allies concluded with certain proposals drafted by Heinrich Lammasch – the last Minister President of imperial Austria, and a member of the Austrian peace delegation in Paris – to modify certain details within the Covenant of the League.[21]

The friendly Allied reply insisted that there had never been any intention of delaying Austria's entry into the League. It would be invited to join as soon as the Peace Treaty was ratified, assuming it had a stable government able to carry out the will of the Covenant. The Allied Powers further recognised the goodwill shown by the republican government of Austria and judged the country's claim for membership to be a strong one. They were also impressed by some of Lammasch's proposals, and would submit these for consideration by the League Council.[22]

The patient Austrian delegation in Paris had to wait even longer for the second tranche of peace terms. As time passed, their anxiety grew, and a typical prisoner psychosis set in amongst some members of the group. They even gave up their walks in the park, as at weekends the Parisians came to gape at them 'like the monkeys in Schönbrunn Park'.[23] The worst affected was the depressive Franz Klein, whose health suffered throughout that summer in Paris, and whose letters were filled with a longing to be reunited with his lover in Vienna. Apparently ignored by the Chancellor (although Renner apologised to Klein for not having involved him more), Klein unsuccessfully tried to persuade Renner to let him go home early in June. He also noted that major differences between the Chancellor's views and those of a majority of the delegation were becoming increasingly difficult to reconcile.[24]

Some of the Austrians were clearly managing to keep their spirits up, as Klein began to grumble about the impromptu music sessions that kept him awake well into the night. Irritated by the incessant piano playing, he moved villas and complained to the revellers that they did not shut their windows. The excuse that came in response was that it was the Chancellor, which drew from Klein the cutting remark, 'This ineradicable servitude! It used to be the Count; now it's just the Social Democrat. But we're still serving and wagging our tails just as we did in the past.'[25]

On 15 June there was an abortive communist putsch in Vienna, in which 12 people died and more than 50 were injured. Renner resisted repeated calls from the Austrian press to return home to deal with the domestic situation, in spite of the fact that there seemed to be no progress in Paris. According to Klein, Renner argued that his presence at St Germain was indispensable, although one of the journalists on the Austrian team believed the Chancellor's decision to stay in France was an astute one, as it absolved him personally of responsibility for the volatile state of affairs in Vienna.[26] Klein was nonetheless highly critical of what he interpreted as the Chancellor's inertia with regard to the events in Paris. On 26 June he wrote that the delegation had heard it might be another fortnight before the remaining terms were delivered, and five or six months before peace was concluded. Klein's appeal to Renner to try to accelerate developments with regard to the Treaty fell on deaf ears: 'He clearly wants to spend as long as possible doing very little, enjoying a comfortable existence; and … in uncertain times he wants to stay out of the firing line and let others get their fingers burned instead.'[28]

> 'The man doesn't want to go home.'
>
> FRANZ KLEIN ON RENNER[27]

Whether Renner could have actually hurried things along is doubtful. The Council spent the first half of June dealing with the German counter-proposals to the Treaty of Versailles and the question of German admission to the League. Then, after the signing of the Treaty on 28 June, Lloyd George left Paris for a short trip to London, while Wilson went back home. In the second week of July, the Council was still requesting additional information on the border area between Austria and Hungary. Some scepticism should also be levelled at the idea that Renner actually *wanted* to prolong his stay in Paris. In correspondence he revealed that the waiting was getting him down; he was keen to return to Vienna where he felt he was needed.[29]

The most noteworthy event in the Austrian camp during the long delay was a change in the catering arrangements. The landlady responsible for the delegation's food had started to cut corners, with the result that the quality of the fare had deteriorated perceptibly. In short, the Austrians felt that she was conning them. From mid-July onwards, they obtained their meals instead from a top-flight Parisian restaurant which, as Renner commented to his wife, made the cuisine at Vienna's exclusive Hotel Sacher look like peasant food.[30] Franz Klein also noted the improvement in quality, but bemoaned the smaller portions. He found himself constantly hungry and soon lodged a complaint, arguing that the old system had been better.[31]

At the same time Otto Bauer was setting out a programme for stronger economic ties between Germany and Austria, as a prelude to an eventual political union. Somewhat alarmed by the noisy Anschluss agitation coming from a sizeable proportion of the German Parliament, Bauer was nonetheless hopeful that Anschluss negotiations might be resumed after the signing of the Austrian peace. As before, however, the German government was of quite a different mind from the parliament; it rejected Bauer's plans, claiming that all moves towards a union in the near future were premature. This rebuttal, combined with the realisation that he could never win the confidence of the Entente Powers, prompted Bauer to plan his political exit. Now that his foreign policy had hit a brick wall, he sent a letter of resignation to Renner in Paris.[32]

The second draft of the Austrian Treaty was handed over on 20 July 1919. This had taken into consideration the Austrians' observations concerning the original peace terms, and contained revisions. In fact, the new document signalled some improvements for Austria, giving the delegation the consolation that not all their work had been in vain. The frontier with Czechoslovakia was amended slightly in Austria's favour around the town of Gmund in the north. As far as the Austro-Yugoslav border was concerned, the Allies agreed that a plebiscite should be held in the Klagenfurt basin. This took place in October 1920 and produced a comfortable majority in favour of remaining with Austria. The treaty revisions also made provision for the German strip of western Hungary, including Ödenburg and the Neusiedlersee, to be joined to Austria without a referendum. This meant that Austria was the only defeated country to leave the Paris Peace Conference with a territorial gain.

The German strip of western Hungary (German speakers made up about three-quarters of the population), which the Treaty of St Germain assigned to Austria, was scheduled to join the Republic as the Burgenland in August 1921. Hungarian paramilitary forces resisted the Austrian occupation, however, and only backed down in the face of threats by the Entente Powers. In December 1921 a plebiscite was held in the area around Ödenburg (Hungarian: Sopron) which voted to remain part of Hungary. The Burgenland is Austria's third smallest province.

Other new features of the Treaty included authorisation to maintain a professional army, limited to 30,000 men, and the regulation of the transferral of Austrian territories to Italy. Reparations had not been touched upon in the original draft; now it was confirmed that Austria would have to pay compensation for the losses and damage suffered by the Allied Powers during the War. This included reparation in kind for the material losses suffered by the areas that the Monarchy had invaded. As an advance on the material compensation, Austria was ordered to deliver around 15,000 cattle to Italy, Serbia and Romania, as well as 1,000 draught horses and 1,000 sheep.

The sum that Austria would be required to pay as financial

compensation was not mentioned in the Treaty; a reparations commission would be established to work out an appropriate figure and a schedule of payments to be discharged within 30 years. It was acknowledged that Austria's resources would not permit it to make complete reparation, but it would have to compensate for damage done to Allied civilians and their property along the same lines as detailed in the German treaty. A special section within the reparations clauses, meanwhile, made provision for the return of artefacts in possession of the Habsburgs, if these had been obtained illegally. Such objects included the Tuscan crown jewels, a Madonna by Andrea del Sarto, some 12th-century items made for the Norman Kings of Sicily, scores of manuscripts pilfered from Naples in 1718, and a golden cup which had belonged to the Polish King Ladislaus IV.[33]

Despite the minor territorial rectifications, overall the revised Treaty represented scant progress for Austria. Even *The Times* felt that the obligations imposed by the Treaty were 'overwhelming' and admitted that the new Republic was starting life as a 'bankrupt state'.[34] Klein wrote that the reaction of the delegation to the terms was as if a bomb had exploded. The Chancellor, he observed, sighed for five minutes and then started talking feverishly, as if this might provide some comfort. The Austrian finance representatives who had come to Paris a month earlier, chiefly the directors of big banks, trembled with fear. They could see the entire financial system about to crumble, precipitated by a run on the banks.[35]

Predictably, the reaction back home was also one of dismay. The *Reichspost*, for example, called it the 'Discord of St Germain',[36] and Renner said of the document: *Although it is possible to see the Entente's willingness to grasp Austria's situation, the result is merely that the death penalty has been replaced by a sentence of voluntary suicide.*[37] He returned to Feldkirch and, together with other leading Social Democrats, decided on a new course for negotiations. The delegation's strategy from now on would be to accept all the boundary changes and the ban on Anschluss, but concentrate on reducing the economic sanctions. With the unanimous approval of the Austrian Parliament, Renner himself took over Bauer's portfolio, thereby strengthening his political position in Austria. *The Times* suggested that Bauer's actions may have been responsible for the severity of the peace terms. The change in Foreign Minister might thus be to Austria's advantage, assuming it had not come too late.[38]

In its reply to the revised peace terms the Austrian delegation emphasised that it only sought changes to the Treaty which were absolutely necessary for the country's survival and to prevent further misery and anarchy. There was no mention of Anschluss, but again there was criticism of the subjection of millions of Germans to foreign rule: 'In vain have we cited the nationality principle that the Great Powers invoked as their war aim, in vain the right of the peoples to self-determination.'[39] The note also contained another warning to the Entente not to leave Austria in the lurch: 'It is not for us to make reproaches; we can only make use of the right to protest, decline the responsibility, and leave the consequences to history.'[40]

One month and a further flurry of notes later, the Austrian Chancellor was handed the final text of the Treaty of St Germain, all 246 pages and 381 Articles of it. It was accompanied by a letter to Renner, in which the Allies addressed some of the general points that the Austrian delegation had made over the summer. The argument repeatedly advanced concerning the accountability of the Austrian people was fundamentally wrong, it said; in the eyes of the Allies, the Austrians and Hungarians shared the responsibility for the ills of the previous five years. The Austrian delegation, the letter continued, had attempted to shift all blame to the Habsburg dynasty, and thus absolve the people from acts committed by its government whose seat was in its capital. In the period leading up to the War, the Allies contested, the Austrians had done nothing to combat the prevailing spirit of militarism. Later, there had been no discernible protest against the War or a refusal to support the Empire's rulers. On the contrary, the War had been greeted with great enthusiasm, and the Germans of Austria had been its chief partisans.

The Allied letter further argued that the War had been fought to shore up German and Magyar supremacy in the Dual Monarchy. The other peoples had not been afforded equal treatment under the imperial regime, and one of the tragedies of the War was that millions of men of the subject peoples had been 'forced, under penalty of death, to fight against their will in the ranks of an army which served at the same time to perpetuate their own servitude and to accomplish the destruction of the liberty of Europe'. The dismemberment of the Monarchy, the Allies asserted, was a logical outcome of this policy of subjugation, and naturally caused serious damage to Austria's economy – 'Whose fault was this?' the letter implied. On the other hand, the Allies underlined the fact that they did not want to aggravate the situation in Austria, and promised to do all they could to assist its recovery.

The final draft of the Treaty again brought some slight revisions in Austria's favour. The Allies had noted Austria's protests concerning the town of Bad Radkersburg, and had sanctioned its transferral from Czechoslovakia. A further territorial change was that all the Styrian communes on the left bank of the River Mur were declared to be part of Austria. As for the South Tyrol, the Allies remarked how for decades the Italian people had been under threat from Austria-Hungary's military command of the plains. In view of this, it seemed judicious to grant Italy's request that the frontier should be the natural one of the Alps, which would offer it a far greater level of security. Other modifications included the provision that Article 88 – the ban on Anschluss – could be overturned in the future by a League of Nations resolution. But the most significant concessions were economic, including a commitment to restore property to Austrian nationals in territories ceded to the successor states. Provision was also made to ensure deliveries of coal from Czechoslovakia and Poland, in return for raw materials.[41]

The Entente made it clear that these were the definitive peace terms – there could be no more negotiation and no more changes. The Austrian delegation had five days to agree to sign the Treaty in its current form, otherwise the armistice of 3 November 1918 would be considered at an end. Renner requested from Clemenceau – and was granted – an extra two days, as he needed to return to Vienna to gain the approval of the National Assembly. The Austrian Parliament duly passed the Treaty, with only the Pan-German deputies voting against. But it was a reluctant approval; in giving its assent the House also registered its protest against the Treaty which, it declared, had 'deprived the Austrian population of its right to self-determination and denied it the right to realise its ardent desire for union with the German mother country'. The protest note also hoped that once peace had dissipated the spirit of 'animosity and national rancour provoked by the

War', the Entente would lift its objection to German unity and sanction Anschluss through the instrument of the League of Nations.[42]

With the authorisation of the Austrian Parliament in his pocket, Renner returned again to Paris. At 11 a.m. on 10 September 1919, he put his name to the Treaty of St Germain, thereby wrapping up a process that had dragged on the length of the summer. In an interview afterwards, he continued in the same modest tone he had adopted throughout the Peace Conference, mixing optimism for the future with flattery for his hosts: *If France lends us aid, the name of St Germain will soon evoke in our hearts feelings which will alleviate the bitterness of the hour we have just passed.* Renner praised France as a magnificent country, singling out the peasantry and the press for particular admiration. He then declared that Austria as a country could not hate; it always respected the opponent it had to fight.[44]

> 'We are the conquered. Yet, misfortune has given us liberty; freed us from the yoke of a dynasty whence for three generations no man of worth has sprung; freed us from the bonds with nations which were never in understanding with us nor with themselves.'
>
> **RENNER AFTER SIGNING THE TREATY**[43]

Arriving back in Vienna, Renner was met by a large crowd at the station. One man broke through the police cordon, ran up to the Chancellor and, in a thick Viennese accent, rebuked him for having let the Entente dictate terms to him. Renner ought to have told them to 'kiss his arse', the man quipped. The police were about to drag the protester away when Renner stopped them. He turned to the man and, speaking in the same dialect, asked him for his name and address. He then said, *You're right. When there's another war and we lose it, then we need to send the right team to St Germain. You'll come with us next time.* The man chuckled and the crowd erupted with laughter.[45]

It had been a tough four months in Paris, and the end result was a difficult one to stomach for Austrians of all political persuasions. In spite of some minor revisions here and there in the new Republic's favour, the overwhelming feeling was that the Treaty of St Germain had left Austria in an impossible position. Prohibited from entering into political union with Germany, and shut off economically from its neighbours, Austria was totally at the mercy of the Entente Powers and their new creation, the League of Nations.

Renner had the distinction of being the first Prime Minister of both the First and Second Austrian Republics. Here he is on the steps of the Vienna Parliament in 1945, surrounded by Soviet officers.

The Legacy

6
The State that No-one Wanted[1]

The impact of the Treaty of St Germain in Austria was both economic and psychological. It was not the reparations commitments that jeopardised the new Republic – these were a red herring as Austria was unable to pay and never did – but the question of whether it could survive as an independent economic unit in the political structure of a Central Europe that had been refashioned by the Peace Conference. The psychological repercussions of the Treaty were perhaps even more serious. Overall, the impression was that German-Austria had been treated unfairly in Paris. Putting the issue of war guilt to one side, there was widespread indignation that the principle of national self-determination, which was supposed to have underpinned the deliberations of the Conference, had been disregarded as far as the 'Germans' were concerned. Thus two-fifths of the German population of old Austria now found themselves involuntarily under foreign rule, while the desire of two parts of the German nation to join in political union was obstructed. Few Austrians, it seemed, cared much for a country with which they could not identify.

Several studies have concluded that the economic outlook for independent Austria was not as bleak as presumed, and that the situation was only aggravated by a pessimistic attitude amongst politicians, business leaders and the wider population as a whole.[2] In the immediate aftermath of the Peace Conference, however, things did look dire. Another harsh winter approached. Four out of five children in the country were classified as under-nourished; in the capital practically all of them were. As ever, the provinces were miserly in handing over supplies, and food prices continued to rise. *The Times* ran a short article in November highlighting the shortage of both fuel and food in Vienna. The coal supply was so scarce, it reported, that the city's electricity works might grind to a halt. Meanwhile, only one-third of households were receiving their weekly ration; the rest were getting none. Families began gathering their own supplies, leading to devastation in the Vienna Woods. Fences were torn down, benches carried off, and even orchards were plundered for wood.[3] In early December there were food riots in the capital.[4]

In December 1919 Renner was invited back to Paris to discuss the parlous state of his country before the Supreme Council. He was his usual affable self, but his words were deadly serious as he painted a wretched picture of the conditions in Austria: a weekly bread and flour ration in Vienna of 100g, high rates of child mortality, only three days' food supplies in place for the following week, and no money to buy in further food from the West. *No government in the world*, he declared, *can remain in office until it has handed out the last loaf in the country. I shudder to think what will be our reception if we go back empty-handed.* The recent outbreaks of plundering, Renner warned, hinted at the anarchy which might ensue if his mission in Paris were a failure. There was no time, he concluded, to worry about guarantees for any credits advanced by the Allied Powers; Austria needed deliveries of food immediately.[5]

The Chancellor's plea for help did not fall on deaf ears. Although the Council emphasised that a long-term solution to Austria's economic plight was only possible with American aid, it agreed that the Austria of the Peace Treaty must be preserved intact, and so decided on several urgent measures to stave off the implosion of the state. Yugoslavia was to arrange an immediate consignment to Austria of 30,000 tons of cereals, payment for which would be dependent on the speed of delivery. One of the chief obstacles to

> 'This problem has nothing whatsoever to do with economics or politics. It is a perfectly straightforward matter of humanity.'
> RENNER'S PLEA FOR MATERIAL ASSISTANCE, DECEMBER 1919[6]

obtaining food imports was that Austria's national assets, in accordance with the Peace Treaty, were mortgaged as a guarantee for reparations. The Allies now acceded to Renner's request that some of these assets should be released from mortgage to enable Austria to generate its own credits.[7] In addition, Britain pledged to supply Vienna with £260,000 worth of fats and three shiploads of coal.

Renner trumpeted his visit as a success, but Austria's immediate prospects were still pretty dismal. In early 1920 the Chancellor paid a visit to Prague, where he reached a series of agreements with the Foreign Minister Eduard Beneš. The material outcome of these negotiations was fairly thin: Czechoslovakia agreed to a daily delivery of 500 wagons of coal plus a total of 2,500 wagons of sugar spread over a period of two-and-a-half months. But a secret protocol was also signed between Renner and Beneš promising mutual diplomatic

Europe 1923

FINLAND

Petrograd (St Petersburg)

Tallinn
ESTONIA

Riga
LATVIA

LITHUANIA
Vilnius

önigsberg
ST
SSIA

Warsaw   Brest-Litovsk

POLAND   Kiev

Moscow

**UNION OF SOVIET
SOCIALIST REPUBLICS**

est

ROMANIA   Odessa

ade   Bucharest

A   BULGARIA
Sofia

Black Sea

Istanbul

GREECE

Athens

TURKEY

SYRIA

IRAQ

CYPRUS

and political assistance in the case of a threat from Hungary. Both countries promised to observe the terms of the Treaty of St Germain (particularly with regard to the western strip of Hungary that had been transferred to Austria). Although the parties rejected the idea of a Danube confederation, they expressed their desire for closer political cooperation.

The rapprochement with Prague was part of a foreign policy orientation that was largely dictated by the terms of the Treaty, and one which would keep on course throughout the 1920s. The ban on Anschluss and the reliance on the Entente Powers for economic survival meant that Austria was obliged to seek closer relations with all its neighbours, rather than focusing on Germany, in an attempt to end its isolation in Central Europe. In this vein, Renner also accepted a snap invitation in April 1920 to come to Rome. The Italian Prime Minister Francesco Nitti immediately pledged his support for a speedy plebiscite in Carinthia, and made a verbal agreement with Renner to guarantee autonomy to the South Tyrol. When the Anschluss issue came up, however, Nitti refrained from making any encouraging noises. On 12 April Renner and his Italian counterpart concluded a secret treaty. Italy bound itself to respect Austria's territorial integrity, while for its part Austria rejected both a Danubian federation and a Habsburg restoration. Renner's trip also brought economic benefits: Italy was prepared to advance 20,000 tons of flour and corn, even more if necessary. This would help plug the gap before the arrival of American flour that had been promised for March. Italy also granted a breathing space of several years to pay the balance of debts owed to it by Austria.

Renner's foreign policy came under fire from his bourgeois coalition partners who criticised his rejection of revisionism in favour of peaceful relations with neighbouring

states. When the secret protocol of the Czechoslovak agreement became known, he was accused of having sold out
the Sudeten Germans. His visit to Rome, moreover, was not
judged positively by the Austrian press. Italy, after all, had
been the arch-enemy, and Renner was accused of behaving
like a dilettante.[8] Meanwhile, the right wing of the Christian
Social Party increased its contact with the ultra-conservative
faction in Hungary, where Admiral Miklós Horthy had been
appointed Regent on 1 March 1920. This blatantly conflicted
with Renner's policy; he dismissed closer ties with the Horthy
regime because of the controversy over western Hungary.
Although both the Treaty of St Germain and the Treaty of
Trianon (signed in June 1920) stipulated that the region now
belonged to Austria, Hungarian paramilitary units persist-
ently obstructed the administrative takeover of the territory.

Within his own party, Renner continued to attract the criticism which had plagued him in the past. We have already
seen how his pragmatic socialism set him against those on
the left more faithful in their adherence to Marxist theory. At
the party conference in autumn 1919 Max Adler condemned
Renner for thinking like a Chancellor rather than a Socialist.
In his defence Renner again outlined his vision of an evolutionary path to the socialist ideal. He declared his support for
the rights of the individual, and criticised the Soviet regime in
Russia, as well as Béla Kun's short-lived communist dictatorship in Hungary which had collapsed three months earlier.[9]

His own party may have considered him a fair-weather
socialist, but Renner succeeded in passing a raft of social legislation during his short tenure as Chancellor. Like all the
Paris Peace Treaties, that of St Germain included a section
outlining general targets for labour reforms. Austria was
quick to meet these. The first measure undertaken by the

Renner government was the introduction of an unemployment benefit only days after the foundation of the Republic. Following the armistice Austria had to accommodate huge numbers of soldiers returning from the front for whom work simply could not be found. While this dole put a major strain on the state finances, it was considered necessary to avoid serious public disturbances. Initially conceived as an emergency measure consisting of direct payments to the unemployed, it was transformed in 1920 into an unemployment insurance scheme to which employers and employees were obliged to contribute.

Perhaps the most frequently cited reform of this period is the introduction of the eight-hour day. This was trialled in the winter of 1918–19 and restricted at first to factory workers. Initial results of the measure proved inconclusive as the parlous state of Austrian industry allowed most businesses concerned to adapt to the new regulations without much difficulty. In 1920 the eight-hour day was extended to all enterprises – including white-collar workers – combined with a degree of flexibility which set a cap on the *weekly* hours worked, thereby allowing some employees a free Saturday afternoon if they chose to put in longer hours from Monday to Friday. This reform was copied by several of Austria's neighbours.

New regulations were also passed limiting the work that could be done by women and children. For example, now women were not allowed to carry out industrial labour during the first six weeks of pregnancy, while it became forbidden to employ women, or boys between the ages of 14 and 18, for any night work (between 8 p.m. and 5 a.m.). The Children's Employment Law of 1918 banned labour for all those under the age of ten, and those under 12 were only permitted to perform light agricultural work or household duties. All child labour was prohibited in dangerous jobs and a general guideline stipulated that work should not imperil the health or morals of children, or prevent their attending school.

Other measures brought in under Renner included a makeover of health and safety legislation, a tightening of dismissal law, particularly for clerical employees, paid leave for industrial workers amounting to between one and two weeks per year, and an extension of sickness and accident insurance. Legislation also provided for workers' councils which represented workers' interests both politically (analogous to chambers of commerce), and in the workplace, where their function was to further the economic and social welfare of employees and to act as an intermediary between employers and workers.[10]

On 10 June 1920 the coalition between the Social Democrats and the Christian Social Party collapsed. Tension between the partners had been rising for months over issues such as the shape the new constitution should take, and the unchecked growth of armed militias on the left and right. The Christian Socials had also accused Renner of trying to use conditions imposed by the Reparations Commission as an excuse to force through legislation; while the Social Democrats charged the Christian Socials with blocking reforms at any price. The thread finally snapped over a minor issue concerning soldiers' councils, the Social Democratic ministers resigned *en masse*, and the search was on for a new government.

Although many on both sides of the House were glad to see the back of the coalition, it was an untimely breach. The new federal constitution was not scheduled to be finished until autumn, after which fresh elections would be held.

Renner hoped that the two main parties might be brought back together somehow, but failing that he warned against relinquishing power altogether. Bauer, by contrast, favoured a permanent break-up of the coalition; he felt that the socialists had recently lost influence within government. What eventually materialised was what the *Neue Freie Presse* called a 'non-coalition', a typically Austrian solution.[11] Party leaders agreed that the legislative programme had to continue until the completion of the constitution. To this effect a cabinet was formed in which all parties were represented proportionately, but rather than working as a coalition they acted independently in government. The Christian Social Michael Mayr was to be the 'chairman' of this curious body. He declared it to be a non-political government with no united programme; the sole job of the administration was to govern in as unbiased a way as possible until the October elections.[12]

Renner kept his portfolio as Minister for Foreign Affairs, but he was thwarted in his intention to stamp his own ideas on the constitution. Before leaving for the Peace Conference, he had entrusted the jurist Professor Hans Kelsen with the task of drafting a constitution which would establish the state as a federal republic based on parliamentary democracy. The Christian Socials, who were dominant in the provinces, supported a strong degree of federalism, whereas the Social Democrats, whose heartland was Vienna (until 1925 an integral part of Lower Austria), favoured a more centralised state. Renner stood somewhere between these two positions, although his own party saw to it that he was ousted from the all-party supervisory committee. The federal constitution was passed unanimously by the National Assembly on 1 October 1920.

It was by now abundantly clear that St Germain Austria

lacked a cohesive identity to motivate its citizens. The new state was deemed to be an artificial and ahistorical creation of the Allies. By contrast, traditional provincial loyalties were very strong; some *Länder* could trace their political history back to before the arrival of the Habsburgs in the 13th century. In defiance of both the central government in Vienna, and the resolutions of the Peace Conference, several provinces decided to undertake unilateral action which threatened the dismemberment of Austria. We have already seen that, as early as May 1919, Vorarlberg voted overwhelmingly in favour of joining Switzerland. Others followed suit. The Tyrol held a plebiscite in April 1921 – even though Vienna ordered its cancellation – in which 98.9 per cent of voters showed their support for unilateral union with Germany. This prompted Salzburg to announce its own referendum for the following month, which also produced a huge pro-Anschluss majority. A few days later, Styria announced it would hold a vote on 3 July.

The reaction from the Allied camp, particularly France, was unequivocal. The League of Nations, to which Austria had been admitted in December 1920, had held a conference in March 1921 to address the Austrian problem. The result of these talks was that France, Britain, Italy and Japan announced that they would allow their claims against Austria to lapse if all the other states concerned did the same and if Austria turned its assets over to the League. The actions of the *Länder* threatened all possibility of concessions; the Allies insisted that the provinces be brought to heel. Mayr resigned over the referendums, and was replaced by a stronger figure, Johann Schober, Viennese Police President and non-party Chancellor. Despite his sympathies with the Anschluss cause, Schober continued to steer the foreign policy course

set by Renner and adhered to the terms of the Treaty. He succeeded in effecting the cancellation of the Styrian plebiscite,
which brought the maverick actions of the *Länder* to an end.

This policy of compliance reached its zenith under Ignaz
Seipel, who became Chancellor in May 1922. Otto Bauer's
arch rival, and the dominant political force in 1920s Austria,
Seipel was one of the sceptics-in-chief towards Anschluss.
Like Renner, Seipel had written on the nationality issue in the
Habsburg Monarchy. His *Nation und Staat* from 1916 argued
that the nation and state were two distinct concepts, the first
defining a political community, the second a cultural one.
For Seipel the disaggregation of the two concepts informed
his thinking on the Anschluss question. He believed – and
here Seipel was entirely in tune with Renner – that the multinational state was a superior framework for the political
organisation of humanity as it fostered cooperation between
peoples and averted the excesses of nationalism.[13]

Although Seipel attempted to paint a positive picture of
Austria's prospects, like his predecessors he stood teetering
on the edge of a very deep precipice. The country was now
beset by rampant inflation, and Austrian finance was on the
verge of collapse with government income from taxation and
the selling of assets virtually worthless. The real possibility
existed that the state might be divided up between its neighbours, or at least be controlled by an international mandate.[14]
In September, therefore, Seipel presented an appeal to the
League Council in Geneva. He insisted that if the victorious
Powers did not intervene to save Austria it would be a 'serious
blow to the peace treaties'.[15] An agreement was signed on 4
October 1922 whereby Britain, France, Italy, Czechoslovakia
and others guaranteed a loan to Austria of 650 million gold
crowns (£27 million). A number of conditions were placed

on Austria in exchange for this credit, which gave the League considerable control over Austrian finances and economic affairs, and a further clause reconfirmed the prohibition on Anschluss for the duration of the loan, until 1943.

Unlike earlier efforts, the Geneva Protocols did not represent a stop-gap measure, but a scheme which offered longer-term benefits. Economic collapse was averted and the currency was stabilised. In summer 1923 the British Minister in Vienna noted that the Austrian crown had been as stable as the pound or dollar over the past ten months.[16] The country also enjoyed something of an economic recovery, albeit only partial and sluggish. Most importantly, perhaps, the urban population was no longer suffering quite as badly from malnutrition. In 1923 the relief mission of the Society of Friends, which had been running since spring 1919, wound up its operation in Vienna 'in view of the general improvement in the condition of Austria'.[18]

> 'The most terrible humiliation of our nation by the enemies of the German people.'
> RENNER ON THE 1922 GENEVA PROTOCOLS[17]

The Social Democrats nevertheless condemned the Protocols, claiming that Seipel had turned Austria into a financial colony of the Western Powers. Renner, whose own foreign policy had been along similar lines, nonetheless also attacked them. He lamented that the country had been sold off to foreign capitalists and called on his party to oppose unconditionally the government that had taken Austria to Geneva.[19] The reconfirmation of the Anschluss ban also drew criticism. Otto Bauer wrote: 'German-Austria has split with Germany and thrown herself into the arms of the Entente ... In the soul of the bourgeoisie Österreichertum [Austrian-ness] has triumphed over Deutschtum [Germanness].'[20]

In the early years of its life as an independent republic, Austria seemed in a permanently critical condition. Far too weak to attempt any revision of the Peace Treaty, it threw in its lot with the Entente Powers, and only survived thanks to the considerable assistance they provided. In such circumstances it is not a surprise that rump Austria was an unloved entity and that its citizens dreamed of alternative solutions such as Anschluss or a Danube federation. By the beginning of 1923, however, the immediate post-war crisis had passed and prospects were brighter, if only slightly. Renner could look back with pride at his own achievements. Under his Chancellorship the transition period had been effected far more smoothly than in either Germany or Hungary. Important social legislation had been introduced, which served as a blueprint for other states in the region. His intercession with the Allies had initiated a process leading to economic reconstruction, and he had helped bring Austria out of international isolation. But Renner, like his party, was now out of office – the Christian Socials won most seats in the 1920 election and formed a coalition with the Pan-Germans – and would not taste government again until after the Second World War. Within the Social Democratic Party, moreover, Renner had been eclipsed by the more dogmatic Bauer, whose hard-line stance would contribute to the increasing polarisation of the Austrian political scene.

7

Political Schism

The Nationalrat election of October 1923 produced a very similar result to that of three years earlier. The Christian Socials were still the largest party, but just short of an overall majority. They continued to govern with the support of the much smaller Pan-German Party, an arrangement which managed to exclude the Social Democrats permanently from power. Otto Bauer, now indisputably the driving force of the Party, seemed untroubled by this state of affairs. He was unwilling to compromise his Party's principles by co-operating with the conservatives, happy to remain firmly in opposition until, presumably, the Marxist dialectic of world history inevitably brought the promised revolution and swept the Social Democrats back to power.

In this period Renner largely withdrew from the spotlight of Austrian political life. He threw himself into the cooperative movement, campaigning to attract members, and seeking to develop organisations which would allow the working class to provide for itself. He also co-founded a workers' bank – the Arbeiterbank – which began its operations on 1 January 1923, and chaired its governing board. Renner saw the bank as a logical extension of the cooperative movement: it exclusively served workers' interests and did not involve itself in capitalist markets.[1] The decrease in his political responsibilities also gave Renner more time to devote to his family and other interests. Although a workaholic, paradoxically Renner was also what the Germans call a *Genussmensch*: someone who enjoys life's pleasures, a *bon vivant*. There were friends to catch up with, games of cards to play, and evenings of dancing to enjoy. But most of all this socialist loved his very bourgeois existence in the villa at Gloggnitz, surrounded by his family.

When we last heard of Renner's daughter Leopoldine she was still an infant who had just spent the first four years of her life in professional care. After she was returned to her parents, the Renners tried to assuage their guilty feelings by spoiling the girl, focusing all their attention on her (Karl did not follow his parents' example, and stuck at just one child). Their treatment of Leopoldine caused her to become utterly dependent – at the age of 16 her mother still dressed her from head to toe – as well as wasteful and extravagant, which was somewhat of an embarrassment for Renner as a Social Democrat.[2] In 1913 she married a civil engineer called Hans Deutsch, only seven years Renner's junior, with whom she had three children: Hans (born 1915), Karl (1917) and Franziska (1920). Renner doted on his grandchildren, who lived with him and his wife in Gloggnitz, and played an important part in their upbringing. Karl Seitz once complained that as soon as one of the children had the slightest tummy-ache Renner would miss committee meetings to be at their side.[3] For their part, the grandchildren remembered a good-humoured man who never took the pressures of his work home with him, and who always found time for them, no matter how busy he might be.[4]

Renner clearly drew great strength from his family,

especially his wife Luise. Theirs was a long and loving marriage; the couple were reliant on each other and there was a great degree of mutual trust, although this assertion is somewhat undermined by the claims – not fully substantiated – that Renner had a long-term affair with an aristocratic lady named Marie Fedrigotti.[5] Despite these allegations, the Renners were undoubtedly a very close-knit family, and Karl a much-loved husband, father and grandfather. To his chagrin he also suddenly became a much-loved great-uncle; a succession of distant and unfamiliar relatives began to appear, begging for assistance from their prominent and successful kinsman. Renner seemed to be an inexhaustible source of funds for these ne'er-do-wells, but he stopped shelling out when he learned that some of the characters for whom he had acted as a guarantor were up to no good.[6]

Although Austria was no longer staring meltdown in the face, and now appeared to be on the road to economic recovery, the picture was not uniformly rosy. The stabilisation of the economy had brought to an end an export boom, and the country's trade and industry was still pretty moribund, a situation not helped by the fact that its hostile neighbours continued to impose high tariffs and import prohibitions, as well as impede transit.[7] With unemployment also on the increase and the cost of living rising, it was a real struggle to meet the demand to balance the budget as laid down in the Geneva Protocols.

Under Seipel's tenure, moreover, the gulf between the right and left in Austrian political life became ever wider. The 'Cardinal without Mercy' was well known for his antipathy towards socialism, and towards the end of the 1920s he steered an increasingly authoritarian course, camouflaging this with woolly ideas about 'true democracy'. The Social

Democrats did not restrain themselves in their vituperative tirades against the Chancellor, whose parallel responsibility as a prelate they saw as indicative of a worrying growth in the influence of the Catholic Church over political affairs.

The antagonism of the political arena reflected – and no doubt also aggravated – the deep-rooted suspicion bordering on hostility between the peasantry and the industrial working class in Austria. Right-wing paramilitary bands known collectively as *Heimwehr* were formed throughout Austria in the aftermath of the War, armed largely with weapons dumped by soldiers returning from the front. Some of these reactionary forces, commanded by former officers, were involved in clashes in border areas, especially with Yugoslav units in the south-east. Soon, however, they turned their attention to quashing any sign of revolutionary activity. Initially, leadership of the movement came from Bavaria, where a very short-lived Soviet Republic had been ruthlessly crushed in May 1919 by the German army, assisted by the right-wing *Freikorps*. Fear that something similar to the Bavarian experiment – or Béla Kun's Hungarian regime – might emerge in Austria gave great impetus to the development of the *Heimwehr*.

The hostility was not one-sided. Renner highlighted this fact when he addressed the party conference in 1923. He urged the industrial proletariat to show more understanding for other sections of society instead of dogmatically rejecting them with radical slogans.[8] The workers, too, had their own armed units, albeit on a smaller scale than the *Heimwehr*. In 1923–4 these were amalgamated into a single, unified organisation, the *Republikanischer Schutzbund*, under the former Army Minister Julius Deutsch. The *Schutzbund* was not only seen as a counterweight to the right-wing *Heimwehr*, but also to increasing Christian Social influence over the army.

Paramilitary activity became an everyday feature of Austrian life in the inter-war years. Clashes between rival units were common, although in the first half of the 1920s these were pretty minor scuffles often fuelled by plenty of drink. But the breakdown of consensus and the radicalisation of parliamentary activity soon found its echo on the streets. The uniforms, banners, slogans and weapons all took on a more threatening dimension.

Seipel began his second term as Chancellor in October 1926, following a two-year interregnum under the more conciliatory Rudolf Ramek. Concerned that the democratic system was coming under threat from forces both within the government and on the streets, the Social Democrats produced a tough-sounding response. At the party conference in autumn 1926 they launched the Linz Programme, replacing their old manifesto of 1901. This new programme made quite clear that the Social Democrats would defend any attempts by the bourgeois parties to liquidate the republic, by force of arms if necessary. It was, on paper at least, a more radical agenda which also emphasised the class struggle, promoted the overthrow of the capitalist system, and called for the construction of a socialist society. Renner was pleased with the new course, as it seemed to have put an end to the old theoretical arguments; the party had now achieved a solid consensus.[9]

The Linz Programme was like a red rag to the more belligerent factions on the right, however, and they exploited its propaganda potential to the full. Never mind that in the past the Social Democrats had proved themselves a moderate force in practice – what greater proof could there be that the Party was planning full-scale revolution? All measures to contain the Red menace were henceforth justified in the eyes of reactionary elements in Austria. It was not long before this challenge was put to the test.

On 30 January 1927, both the *Schutzbund* and the *Heimwehr*-affiliated *Frontkämpfervereinung* had planned to parade in the village of Schattendorf in the Burgenland. The two paramilitary organisations had developed a bitter rivalry in this part of the country, and clashes were increasingly commonplace, but the events of 30 January took the conflict to a new level. As the *Schutzbund* marched to where a Social Democratic Party meeting was being held, shots were fired into their ranks from inside a village tavern. One man – a wounded war veteran – and an eight-year-old boy were killed; several other marchers were injured. There was no retaliation against this outrage from the *Schutzbund* force.

The Schattendorf affair polarised the Austrian political scene still further. In parliament, Renner rejected the Christian Social claim that the shootings had been a non-political act. The killers, he asserted, were contaminated by the spirit emanating from within their Party, and for this reason the Christian Socials must shoulder a large proportion of the blame for Schattendorf.[10] When it came to the general election of April 1927, the political divide was even more evident: the Christian Social Party, the Pan-Germans, and some small Nazi factions all joined forces in a Unity List. The alliance had the desired result of keeping the left at bay. Although the Social Democrats improved on their 1923 performance, the marginal increase of three seats still left them 12 short of an absolute majority.

On 14 July 1927 the Schattendorf defendants were found not guilty by a Viennese court. When this astonishing verdict – the British Minister in Vienna called it 'appalling'[11] – became known the following morning, workers in Vienna downed tools and marched on Parliament. As *The Times*' Central European correspondent, George Gedye, observed, this was not an uncommon occurrence in 1920s Austria.[12] What made 'the bloody 15 July' different was that the *Schutzbund*, who were normally on hand to ensure that processions took place in a disciplined manner, had not had sufficient time to mobilise their forces before the crowds assembled at the Nationalrat. Neither were the police present in sufficient numbers to help manage the protest. Nonetheless, Gedye states that the demonstration was orderly and perfectly good-tempered until some isolated shots – police revolvers – were heard emanating from behind the Parliament building. The mood changed instantly. Convinced that they were under fire from the security forces, the workers panicked, resulting in one of the bloodiest incidents in Viennese history.[13] A total of 85 civilians and four policemen died that day. The Social Democrats called a general strike which collapsed after three days thanks to the intervention of *Heimwehr* forces.

After the First World War an insignificant National Socialist movement existed in Austria, which was an offshoot of a German nationalist party that had been founded in Bohemia in 1903. After Hitler rebuilt the Nazi Party in Germany, following his early release from prison, one faction of the Austrian National Socialists styled itself the Hitler Movement, and subordinated itself to the German Nazi Party. In 1930 it failed to win enough votes for a seat in Parliament, but two years later made an impressive showing at provincial elections. Banned under Dollfuss, the party continued to operate illegally, and attempted a *coup d'état* in July 1934. After the Anschluss, many leading Austrian Nazis were passed over for positions of responsibility, the jobs being given to Germans. This caused a great deal of bitterness.

The Schattendorf killings and their aftermath made two things very clear. First, the relationship between right and left in Austria, hitherto acrimonious and hostile, had now reached a stage where reconciliation seemed impossible; 15

July paved the way for the brief civil war of 1934. In the eyes of the bourgeois parties the Social Democrats had matched the fiery rhetoric of their Linz Programme with violent insurrection on the streets. But the rioting had been neither organised nor sanctioned by the socialists; both Bauer and Karl Seitz tried ineffectively to pacify the mob from on top of a fire engine before a hail of stones forced them to dive for cover.[14] Much of the extreme behaviour from the protestors that day was either perpetrated or instigated by radical elements outside the Social Democratic Party, while the casualty figures for both sides tell their own story. For their part, the Social Democrats must have considered their fears that the right was heading towards some sort of *coup d'état* confirmed.

The second, and related, point is that the *Heimwehr* and *Schutzbund* were treated very differently by the Austrian government and judiciary. The vast majority of arms in the possession of these two paramilitary organisations were held illegally, but whereas the government was increasingly rigorous in confiscating weapon stocks belonging to the left, it had actually facilitated the build-up of *Heimwehr* armouries. During his first tenure as Chancellor, Seipel had encouraged industrialists to channel money through central government to finance the right-wing paramilitaries.[15] For the conservatives the *Heimwehr* represented an unofficial auxiliary force in the struggle against socialism, and during the unrest of July 1927 various regional outfits worked in tandem with the authorities to prevent left-wing disturbances in the provinces.[16] It is in the light of such high-level backing that the acquittal of the Schattendorf killers must be understood.

Although Renner had welcomed the Linz Programme of 1926, a year later he was warning his party comrades against moving to a position of isolation and hollow posturing. He told the conference: *It is dangerous and contradictory to always talk of revolution and at the same time to acknowledge that it is something not possible to achieve.*[17] Renner was one of the few Social Democrats who believed that cooperation with the Christian Socials was the only way forward after the tragedy of July 1927. The polarisation of Austrian politics, he said, had made the threat of civil war ever more real. For this reason, Renner continued, cool heads rather than radicalisation were needed. He urged the Party not to shy away from the responsibility of government, but actively to seek a share in the running of the country. Bauer, on the other hand, insisted that Seipel's open hostility to the workers excluded any possibility of a coalition. He also argued that cooperation with the class enemy could see the Party lose support to the Communists. Renner's address received warm applause, suggesting that there was a fair amount of support within the party for his pragmatic approach. But the conference ultimately backed Bauer's uncompromising line, and supported the motion that the *Schutzbund* should be developed into a more potent paramilitary force.

In the wake of July 1927, establishment support for the *Heimwehr* came out into the open. Seipel delivered several lectures over the next two years in which he endorsed the *Heimwehr* as a non-party political organisation which reserved its loyalty for the state rather than a particular class. He praised their quest for 'true democracy', a favourite term of his to describe a political set-up that was anything but democratic. Seipel's search for alternatives to the parliamentary system became ever keener towards the end of the decade, and he thought the *Heimwehr* could be a useful tool for implementing his plans. The various provincial organisations – which for the sake of simplicity we have grouped under the name *Heimwehr* – lacked any central leadership, however, and were beset by petty rivalries and jealousies that hindered the unification of the movement. What they shared were a hatred of socialism and a strong dislike for republican government in general. A potent dose of anti-Semitism also characterised the movement's outlook, but this was not uncommon in Austria.

Emboldened by the anti-socialist momentum of the Seipel administration, the *Heimwehr* upped its campaign to sweep away the revolutionary rubbish of the parliamentary system and became hungry for power itself. Within the movement, however, there was division over the form and substance of a post-democratic Austria. A significant proportion of *Heimwehr* members, chiefly from the old officer class, retained a strong attachment to the Monarchy, and thus still harboured dreams of a Habsburg restoration in Austria. Others, including a small but growing number of Nazis, had pan-German sympathies, and were thus strong advocates of Anschluss.

In July 1928 the movement obtained some sort of federal leadership but remained far from united; the various provincial organisations continued to guard their autonomy. Nonetheless, the full force of the *Heimwehr* was brought to bear on the government in 1929 when the question of constitutional changes was under discussion. The right saw this as their chance to establish authoritarian government in Austria, and the *Heimwehr* presented an ultimatum. They demanded far-reaching change and offered to participate in a new cabinet if the government itself felt too weak to implement the reforms.

When the amendments were passed in December 1929 under Schober, back for a second term as Chancellor, the *Heimwehr* were seriously disappointed. Seipel had favoured expanding the powers of the Presidency, including a provision for emergency rule, and removing Vienna's status as a separate province (it would revert to being part of Lower Austria), thus crushing the one remaining socialist bastion in the country. Schober's original bill was very much in the Seipel mould, and was sharply criticised by Social Democratic members of the Nationalrat. Renner argued that the proposals signified a repressive strengthening of state authority and warned that the bill would lead to the emasculation of Parliament.[18] Together with Robert Danneberg, the Social Democrat spokesman for constitutional affairs, he tried to take Schober step by step away from this authoritarian course. Their secret negotiations bore fruit: the reform of the constitution represented a compromise. Vienna retained its status as a *Land*, and the new executive powers were not as extensive as originally drafted. But henceforth the President was to be elected directly by the people rather than Parliament.

The Wall Street Crash of October 1929 ushered in the Great Depression, whose effects were felt as severely in Austria as elsewhere. Exports shrivelled, unemployment rocketed, and the Austrian banking system went into freefall, culminating in the collapse of the Creditanstalt, the country's largest bank, in May 1931. The economic crisis further destabilised the volatile political situation, with six changes of government over a period of three years. The coalition between the bourgeois parties had started to crack, and the Unity List of 1927 was not reconstituted for the November 1930 election. This time the Pan-Germans stood together with the small, peasant-oriented *Landbund*, and consequently the Social Democrats emerged as the largest party for the first time since 1919. They only gained one seat, however, which still left them several short of an overall majority, and the party remained in opposition.

Although the Christian Social Party lost seven seats at the election, this was compensated for by the eight seats gained by the *Heimatblock*, a new political party formed to represent the interests of the *Heimwehr*. It may seem perverse that this paramilitary outfit should want to participate in a process it so tirelessly repudiated, but it must not be forgotten that the National Socialists worked the democratic political system in Germany to great success, only to dismantle it when they had secured their hold on power. The Austrian Nazis, meanwhile, made a respectable showing at the 1930 election. Although they failed to capture a seat, their 100,000 votes were five times as many as polled by the Austrian Communists.

In private Renner admitted that the heightened political tension was adversely affecting his health. He was putting on weight again and suffering from liver problems; sometimes he felt scarcely able to breathe, he said. He was also concerned that he was neglecting his writing.[19] Financial concerns compounded Renner's worries. At the end of the 1920s the villa in Gloggnitz was renovated, while considerable sums had to be expended to prop up his son-in-law's business. When this went bankrupt, Renner was forced to borrow money to support his daughter's family.

After a number of years taking a back seat politically, Renner was ready to return to a more prominent position at the start of the 1930s. As the Social Democrats had emerged from the 1930 election as the largest party, it fell to them to provide the post of Speaker in the Nationalrat. Initially the Party selected a friend of Renner's, Matthias Eldersch, for the job. When Eldersch died suddenly in April the following year, Renner was elected to replace him.

In June 1931, Otto Ender's government fell in the wake of the Creditanstalt collapse, and the hopeless failure of a customs union project with Germany. The latter was negotiated in secret and took European governments by surprise. France and the Little Entente countries – Czechoslovakia, Romania and Yugoslavia, who had formed an alliance under French tutelage as a protection against both Hungarian irredentism and a Habsburg restoration – saw the customs union as a clandestine first step towards Anschluss, and immediately raised a storm of protest. When Austria was warned that any such plans would jeopardise further international loans, the project was soon shelved.

Politically the country now found itself at something of an impasse, as the disintegration of the customs union scheme had strained the relationship between the Christian Socials and Pan-Germans still further. Seipel, who had been pulling strings behind the scenes in the two years since his resignation, now came up with an extraordinary suggestion: he offered the Social Democrats a share in government, with Otto Bauer as Vice-Chancellor. The Socialists' flat refusal to cooperate with Seipel has often been criticised as a missed opportunity, and symptomatic of the party's misplaced idealism in the inter-war era. But this assessment must be qualified. Given Seipel's well-documented shift towards

The impetus towards a customs union between Austria and Germany actually came from Berlin. A paper prepared for the German Foreign Office in July 1930 insisted that union with Austria ought to be a top priority, as it would open up new possibilities for Germany and establish it as a presence in the Danube basin. A customs union, disguised in a pan-European cloak, would be the first step towards Anschluss. Chancellor Schober could not resist the invitation; he did not think Austria capable of making an economic turnaround on its own. Although it was chiefly French opposition that put an end to the scheme, in private many Austrian businessmen feared that the country's technological backwardness *vis-à-vis* Germany would make its industry uncompetitive. Christian Social politicians may also have worked secretly to scupper the project.

authoritarian solutions, his proposal cannot have been motivated by a desire to protect the democratic structure of the
Republic. It was far more likely that this was a ploy to induce
the Social Democrats to shoulder some of the responsibility
for the mess the country found itself in. It was no surprise that
Bauer rejected Seipel's offer, but Renner was not in favour of
the plan either. Although a share of power was something he
had urged the party to work towards in the 1920s, he felt the
country needed a government composed of moderate, conciliatory figures, which Seipel and Bauer were not.

Government in Austria stuttered on with another Chris-
tian-Social-led administration under Karl Buresch which,
besides the mounting economic problems, had to deal with a
putsch attempt by the Styrian *Heimwehr* in September 1931,
as well as friction within the cabinet over the 'German question' which ultimately led to the withdrawal of Pan-German
support. Elections to choose the Federal President were scheduled for the autumn of 1931 on the basis of the constitutional
amendments of 1929. Renner was chosen by his party to fight
the election and undertook an exhausting campaign which
saw him speak at as many as 50 mass meetings. His health
suffered again; he started to experience bouts of asthma
and catarrh which he tried to fight off with nicotine. In the
end his campaigning was futile; due to the volatile domestic
atmosphere the parties decided against going through with
the public vote, and opted to revert to the previous arrangement whereby the ballot for President was undertaken by the
elected politicians. Although on paper Renner stood a better
chance in a popular vote, in fact the parliamentary poll was
much closer than expected; he only lost to the incumbent,
Wilhelm Miklas, by 93 to 109 votes.

In Germany, of course, the main beneficiary of the Great

Depression were the Nazis, who from almost nowhere became the second-largest party at the 1930 elections, and then trounced the Social Democrats in July 1932, winning 37 per cent of the vote. Renner mistakenly imagined that the appeal of the Nazi movement would remain limited in Austria, convinced that both the bourgeoisie and working class were immune to its charms. *No prophet is venerated in his homeland*, he confidently asserted.[20] In the Austrian provincial elections of April 1932, however, the Nazis polled between 10 and 15 per cent, while the Pan-German vote collapsed completely. The new government which was formed under the diminutive Engelbert Dollfuss in May 1932 was a Christian Social-*Heimwehr* coalition with a majority of just one seat in Parliament.

Dollfuss would be the last democratic Chancellor and first dictator of inter-war Austria. Seen by many as Seipel's political heir, his time in office represented the culmination of a process that had begun with the break-up of Renner's coalition government in 1920. Throughout Europe in this period there was deep mistrust of Marxist parties, fuelled by the events of the Russian Revolution and the fear that Bolshevism might spread. But the collapse of the democratic consensus in 1920s Austria was also in part due to an immaturity shown by figures from across the political spectrum. In imperial Austria, elected representatives had enjoyed status without responsibility, office without power; ultimately all decision-making had been in the hands of the Emperor and his government. When these same politicians finally had real authority in the republican period, many failed to use it wisely. The lack of responsibility on the part of both government and opposition figures was exacerbated, moreover, by the consequences of the Paris Peace Conference, which meant that both economic and foreign policy in Austria were dictated to a significant extent by the Entente Powers and the League of Nations. When, in summer 1932, Dollfuss negotiated another League loan for Austria, the price was a further prohibition on political or economic union with Germany, and renewed international control over the Austrian economy.

8
Democracy Eclipsed

Dollfuss was a formidable statesman who did not shy away from political conflict, and who remained unfazed by the opposition stacked up against him on both the left and right. It was he who finally implemented the authoritarian course dreamed of by Seipel, and who boldly squared up to the National Socialists both at home and in Germany, until the failed Nazi putsch of July 1934 ended in his assassination. Dollfuss apologists paint him as the great Austrian patriot whose liquidation of parliamentary democracy was not the result of some master plan, but had been forced on him by a system which had ceased to function. In their defence they cite the offer of a coalition Dollfuss made to the Social Democrats. As we have seen with Seipel, such a proposal was no proof of democratic convictions.

What remains uncontested, however, is that democracy came to an end in Austria following a bizarre series of events in which Karl Renner, as Speaker in Parliament, played a leading role. In February 1933, a conflict between workers' and employers' representatives erupted, culminating in a 72-hour strike by the strongest socialist trade union, the railway workers. The government wanted to come down hard on the strikers (Dollfuss was a former Director-General of the Austrian railways), and so summoned an extraordinary sitting of Parliament to discuss disciplinary measures. During the vote there was a heated argument between Christian Socials and Pan-Germans, and Dollfuss's government, with its gossamer majority, seemed on the verge of collapse. To cool things down, Renner suspended the sitting for ten minutes, during which Bauer, Seitz and Danneberg tried to encourage him to step down as Speaker of the House so he could cast a vote for the opposition.

When the voting slips had been counted, it emerged that the government had lost by 80 votes to 81. But there was a question over the validity of one of the voting slips. The problem was that two of the Socialist papers carried the same name – Simon Abram – whereas there was none for his comrade and neighbour and in the House, Wilhelm Schieben. Although Renner declared that everything was in order – it was obvious to all that both men must have taken part – the Christian Socials protested angrily; they insisted that one of the two slips be declared invalid. At this point Renner said it was impossible for him to continue in his role as Speaker if such a large proportion of the House contradicted his decisions. He stepped down, and thus was free to vote with the opposition. This was not simply a spontaneous decision, but a tactic the Social Democrats had been mulling over for a while, given how close voting had become in Parliament.

What the socialists had not foreseen was that the Christian Social Deputy Speaker of the House, the ex-Chancellor Rudolf Ramek, would also resign his office to vote with the government. When the third Speaker of the House, the Pan-German Joseph Straffner, followed suit, Parliament ground to a halt: it could not function without a Speaker. The bemused delegates hung around in the building for a while, unsure of what to do, before filing out scratching their heads. Renner's grandson, Karl, who had been watching the events unfold that day, recalled how phlegmatic his grandfather had been immediately afterwards: 'I went into Grandfather's office. He said, "Let's go home and have lunch."' [1] Although his grandson's memory here must be somewhat rusty – it was, in fact, ten o'clock at night – the reaction was indicative of how Renner stuck to the normal rhythms of life even in the worst of crises. On the drive back to his house that evening, Renner is alleged to have said, *Well ... I never expected that to happen.*[2]

Neither can Renner have expected that 4 March 1933 would be the last day of democratic government in Austria for more than 12 years. On 9 March he issued a statement insisting that Parliament had not been crippled and denying that it was incapable of functioning. Any attempt to bypass the constitutional workings of Parliament was invalid, he added. On 15 March there was a last futile attempt by the opposition MPs to re-elect the Nationalrat speakers, but Dollfuss signalled his intentions by sending 200 criminal police officers to the Parliament building, with more police and troops as back-up. The sitting lasted no more than ten minutes.

The Social Democrats had been anticipating a conservative *coup d'état* for some years. And yet, when the time came, they found themselves unprepared and impotent against the forces of reaction. Renner once again demonstrated his astonishing adaptability by trying to devise a mechanism which might place Dollfuss's actions within a legal framework. This scheme would give the Chancellor power to rule by decree, but allow a parliamentary committee to supervise government decisions. Renner the socialist even set about drafting a corporate constitution of the sort the *Heimwehr* had been demanding for years. He also, with the full backing of his party, offered to enter into negotiations with Dollfuss. At the 1933 party conference, the moderate Social Democrats won the day, with Renner arguing that it would be suicidal to lead the radicalised but unprepared working class into outright conflict against the right. Nonetheless, the extent to which he was willing to work for an accommodation with proto-fascism in 1933 was remarkable, and presaged his public approval of Anschluss in 1938, as well as his endorsement of the dismemberment of Czechoslovakia some months later.

Dollfuss rejected Renner's approaches. Bolstered by the full support of Mussolini – who paraded himself as Austria's protector in the face of Nazi threats and also urged the Austrian government to liquidate socialism as quickly as possible – and with the *Heimwehr* more or less on board, Dollfuss ignored calls to reactivate Parliament, and ran the country using an old imperial law from 1917 – which had passed untouched into the republican constitution – giving the government the right to rule by decree. Dollfuss used these emergency powers from wartime to suspend the constitution, ban political meetings, and put through a raft of financial and economic measures. At the end of March 1933 another decree banned the *Republikanischer Schutzbund*, provoking no reaction from the socialist paramilitaries.

In an attempt to fill the void left by the suspension of political life, and to counterbalance the ever-increasing support for National Socialism in Austria – following the Nazi triumph in Germany, government circles in Vienna felt that they could not risk new elections – Dollfuss launched a patriotic campaign in May 1933, announcing the creation of the *Vaterländische Front* (Fatherland Front). The Front was conceived by the government as a replacement for the political parties who since the dissolution of Parliament were deemed superfluous. Initially this organisation was little more than a glorified propaganda machine, spouting criticism of the Social Democrats and National Socialists – both declared to be enemies of the state. It also promoted a new Austrian consciousness based on the traditional formula that the Austrians were a German people whose particular history and 'mission' in Central Europe had placed them at the head of the German nation. National Socialism was derided as a thoroughly un-German phenomenon, with its roots in 'Slavic' Prussia. With the Nazi takeover of Germany, so the propaganda went on, Austria was the only place where the 'true soul' of Germanness survived.

On 12 February 1934, units of the now-illegal *Schutzbund* resisted a police search for weapons at a workers' club in Linz, locking the officers in a cellar. When police reinforcements arrived the *Schutzbund* forces returned fire, unleashing a bloody, three-day civil war. A general strike was proclaimed throughout the country, and martial law imposed in Vienna. Karl Seitz, the capital's Mayor, was dragged from the town hall along with other Social Democratic councillors. A barbed-wire barrier was constructed around central Vienna, with machine-gun posts dotted around the perimeter. Meanwhile, police and *Heimwehr* detachments tried to force their way into the workers' huge, fortress-like housing estates in the suburbs, where secret arms caches had been bricked up for just such an eventuality. Some tenement complexes were taken almost immediately, before the weapons could be retrieved. Others held out, and Dollfuss took the decision to employ the army and heavy artillery against the besieged workers.

By 15 February the fighting had come to an end.

Government figures suggested that the workers suffered 137 dead and 399 wounded, whereas their own losses were 102 killed and 309 injured. George Gedye called these figures 'quite ridiculous', insisting that the socialist casualties were far higher.[3] The Social Democratic Party was immediately outlawed, and its political control of Vienna – both province and municipality – was terminated. The *Heimwehr* flag was hoisted over the town hall. Even before the main fighting had broken out political leaders on the left, including Renner, had been arrested, although Bauer and Deutsch managed to escape to Brno in Czechoslovakia. Now around 10,000 Social Democrats throughout the country were rounded up. Nine of these would later be executed, the death penalty recently having been reintroduced in Austria.

Renner spent a total of three months in custody, mostly imprisoned in a small cell (3.2m by 2.75m). And yet he suffered far less from incarceration than his party colleagues Seitz and Danneberg. His spirit remained unbroken by the experience, his optimism undefeated. After two months in prison he sent his granddaughter Franziska a poem about his daily routine, which made it sound as if he were on holiday. His only grumbles, he wrote to his wife, were that he was losing time and putting on weight again: *I eat out of boredom; I eat because there's nothing to do here but digest food. I'm hungry all the time*.[4] The thing he missed most of all was peppers, which he had his grandson smuggle into the jail. When Bauer, in exile, heard of this he could not believe his ears: 'Damn Renner and his peppers! Demanding peppers at such a time!'[5]

When Renner was released in May 1934 he remained under surveillance. His telephone was cut off and he was forbidden to use his car. For a while the family was forced to move to an apartment in Vienna which, although fairly spacious, was not ideal for three generations of one family. Eventually they were permitted to return to the villa in Gloggnitz. Although Renner occasionally met up with party colleagues, he refrained from taking part in any clandestine political activity. He told a young Bruno Kreisky (Social Democrat Chancellor of Austria 1970–83) that after operating to the letter of the law for 40 years he could not suddenly go underground.[6]

The Austrian Nazi Party had already been declared illegal a year earlier, after a wave of terrorist attacks. Hitler always maintained publicly that Germany had nothing to do with National Socialist activity on Austrian soil, and yet broadcasts from Munich continually denounced the Dollfuss government, predicting an imminent political and economic collapse, while Austrian Nazis were encouraged to engage in acts of civil disobedience. An Austrian Legion was also formed in Bavaria from Austrian National Socialists who had fled over the border. This force, which was armed and given military training by the Nazis, grew to 15,000 men, and engaged in cross-border skirmishes and acts of sabotage. Meanwhile, the underground Nazi movement in Austria continued to gain adherents.

The battle-lines between Austro-Fascism and Nazism were not always clear; even Dollfuss had considered bringing some National Socialists into the government as late as May 1933. Quite apart from the obvious ideological elements the two movements shared, a large number of those supposedly in the patriotic camp were equivocal about their affiliations. This ambivalence is best personified by the *Heimwehr* leader and Vice-Chancellor Prince Starhemberg. We have seen how two major strands existed in the *Heimwehr*: one German-national in outlook, and thus pro-Anschluss; the other legitimist (monarchist), and so more patriotic. The kindest assessment one can make of Starhemberg was that he was confused; more realistically he was an opportunist *par excellence*. So although this charming but thoroughly unreliable individual harped on to his legitimist friends about his commitment to the cause of Austrian independence, and also headed the patriotic campaign as leader of the Fatherland Front, in truth he kept in contact with Berlin and left his options open. Throughout the wider ranks of the *Heimwehr*, a large proportion of the German nationalists switched their allegiance to National Socialism when the Pan-German Party disintegrated, and thus represented a potential Trojan Horse in the event of any Nazi coup attempt. On the many occasions when *Heimwehr* and Nazi forces came to blows in mid-1930s Austria, the quarrel was less about a clash of political philosophies and more about who would be in control. Substantial evidence exists to show that some *Heimwehr* leaders would have been happy to see a National Socialist coup in Austria if this were a route to power and they were allowed to run the show

On 1 May 1934, Dollfuss published a new constitution for Austria which established the country as a *Ständestaat* (corporate state). Inspired by a number of sources, including Mussolini's Italy, a papal encyclical from 1931, and the

Ernst Rüdiger von Starhemberg (1899–1956) came from an old Austrian aristocratic family. A playboy with a keen sense of adventure, Starhemberg served in the German *Freikorps* in the early 1920s, and also took part in Hitler and Ludendorff's abortive Beer Hall Putsch of 1923. He then returned to Austria and rose to become the federal leader of the *Heimwehr* in 1930. Through the strength of the movement, Starhemberg was brought into government and became Vice-Chancellor in May 1934. His precise dealings with the Nazis remain unclear, but much of his autobiography is whitewash. Starhemberg fled Austria after Anschluss, fought briefly on the Allied side, and emigrated to Argentina in 1942, where he lived until his death.

theories of the corporate state taught by Professor Othmar Spann at Vienna University, this was an attempt to restructure political representation based on *Stände* or professions. Thus each professional group within society would elect a number of representatives to the various councils established to advise the government. As the corporate state was never fully implemented, discussion of it need delay us no longer; suffice to say that the position of the Executive, and the Chancellor in particular, was strengthened considerably. Overall the May constitution gave Dollfuss licence to continue ruling the country with an iron hand.

The formal unveiling of the Austro-Fascist regime triggered another wave of Nazi terrorist activity. But Dollfuss stood firm, as did Mussolini when Hitler paid him a visit in mid-June, urging the Italian dictator to bring about the removal of the dogged Austrian Chancellor. Then, on 25 July 1934, the Austrian National Socialists made their long-anticipated strike. Although the Nazi putschists assassinated Dollfuss – which may or may not have been a direct aim of the coup – the rest of their operation met with little success. The Austrian security forces had got wind of the plot to seize President Miklas, and so were able to intercept the kidnappers. He was duly able to appoint Kurt von Schuschnigg, the Justice Minister, as Dollfuss's successor. A plan to take control of the Austrian radio network was also thwarted. Mussolini, meanwhile, backed up his strong words by sending Italian troops to the Brenner Pass as a warning to Germany against an invasion. Just how much the Führer was involved in the planning for the July putsch is unclear, but it seems unlikely that he was ignorant of the plot altogether.

Kurt von Schuschnigg, 36 years old when he became Chancellor, was a more reserved individual than Dollfuss, his scholarly demeanour reinforced by the round-rimmed spectacles that were a permanent feature atop his thin nose. A quiet and pious man, he lacked the charisma of his predecessor but not his toughness; after all, it was Schuschnigg as Justice Minister who saw to it that death sentences were handed out to nine socialists after the February revolt. Nor did Schuschnigg have any compunction about sending the leaders of the Nazi putsch to the gallows, even though these had been promised safe passage to the German border if they surrendered. He also eventually neutered the *Heimwehr*, first by ensuring that the organisation was as embedded as tightly as possible in the Fatherland Front, and then by dissolving it for good in 1936.

Schuschnigg harboured fairly strong monarchist sympathies, and there were times in the years leading up to Anschluss when he toyed with the idea of a Habsburg restoration as a possible, if not altogether realistic scheme to counter the growing pressure from Nazi Germany. His nostalgia for Austria's imperial past did not, however, alter his conviction that his compatriots were a German people; it would never have occurred to Schuschnigg to put clear blue water between the two Central European neighbours by proclaiming the birth of the Austrian nation. As we have explained, the Austrian mind of the inter-war years was clearly stamped with the hallmark of Germanness, and conditioned by a cultural rather than political conception of national consciousness, which made support for union with Germany only natural.

While Mussolini continued to strut up and down the European stage in the guise of Austria's protector, Schuschnigg was fairly secure in his position. What is more, the Austrian economy gradually improved from 1934 onwards, although unemployment remained a thorny issue. But after the scandal

of Italy's Abyssinian adventure of 1935–6, in which Mussolini invaded and conquered a fellow member of the League of
Nations, and the widespread censure it brought, the Italian
dictator needed an important friend in Europe. There was
really only one candidate. Just as Mussolini's subsidies to the
Heimwehr stopped, so did his sabre-rattling in Germany's
direction. The Friendship Treaty followed in October 1936,
heralding the start of the Rome-Berlin Axis and the end of
unqualified support for Austrian independence.

In the wake of the failed putsch attempt of July 1934,
German policy towards Austria changed to an evolutionary
path towards Anschluss. To that end Hitler sent Franz von
Papen, who had been forced to resign as German Vice-Chancellor, to Vienna as ambassador. From noble Catholic stock,
and not a paid-up member of the Nazi Party, von Papen could
appear to Schuschnigg as the respectable face of Germany.
He used his wily charms and well-honed diplomatic skills
on the Austrian Chancellor to negotiate the July 1936 agreement, on the face of it a document normalising relations
between Austria and Germany. By the terms of the agreement Germany promised to respect Austrian sovereignty, and
refrain from meddling in its internal affairs (National Socialism in Austria was deemed to be a purely Austrian concern).
For its part Austria was to conduct its policy in accordance
with the principle that it recognised itself to be a German
state – a clause which clearly aligned Austria's foreign orientation to that of Germany. What was not made public was an
additional protocol: the secret 'Gentlemen [*sic*] Agreement',
whose terms were much less favourable for Austria. A total
of nine clauses offered far-reaching concessions to Germany,
including an amnesty for all Nazi prisoners in Austria except
those guilty of very grave crimes, and a promise that two

German nationalists (crypto-Nazis) be admitted to the government at some appropriate point in the near future. The two governments were also compelled to restrain their media from reporting negatively about the other country.

George Gedye called the July agreement, with its additional protocol, 'Austria's death-warrant'.[7] The British Foreign Office, which was unaware of the secret clauses, thought it a success, although much would depend on whether Germany adhered to the letter and spirit of the agreement.[8] At all events the Western democracies had shown by their inaction over Hitler's reoccupation of the Rhineland a few months earlier that they were already on the path of appeasement and might not be prepared to go as far as war to defend Austrian independence. Ever more isolated internationally, Schuschnigg had two realistic options (discounting a Habsburg restoration as fantasy): to work for an accommodation with Germany, or seek to repair the relationship with the working class, which had been shattered by the events of February 1934. The Chancellor, a prisoner of his convictions, chose to steer the German course, thereby admitting Nazism by the back door.

> 'German-Austria must return to the great German motherland ... people of the same blood belong in the same Reich.'
> ADOLF HITLER, *MEIN KAMPF*

Over the next 18 months the Austrian National Socialists were able to promote their cause with far more freedom than before. They received the same lenient treatment from the police that the *Heimwehr* had enjoyed in the past, although there was no repeat of the terrorist campaign of 1933–4. By early 1938, however, Hitler had grown impatient at the lack of progress on the Austrian question, and resolved to settle it without further delay. That February, therefore, he invited

– or rather ordered – Schuschnigg to his mountain retreat above Berchtesgaden. Once there, Schuschnigg was subjected to one of the Führer's famous tirades. Hitler accused the Chancellor of oppressing and torturing 'his' people (i.e. the Austrian Nazis) in Austria for years, and for violating the terms of the July agreement. He handed the Chancellor a document and, spitting with rage, threatened immediate invasion if Schuschnigg refused to sign. Just to make things more uncomfortable for his visitor, he refused to allow him to smoke and surrounded him with three top German generals.

After lunch, which took place in absolute silence, Hitler relented and allowed Schuschnigg a single cigarette. The Chancellor then proceeded to chain-smoke throughout the rest of his ordeal until 9 p.m. He retained his composure and quietly told Hitler that he could only agree to three of the 11 points; the remainder needed the consent of President Miklas. Still, Schuschnigg made pretty substantial concessions: the surrender of the Ministries of the Interior and State Security to Nazi sympathisers; an amnesty for all National Socialist prisoners in Austria, including terrorists and murderers; and the opening of the Fatherland Front to the Nazis on the basis of full equality. The Austrian government was given three days to yield to the rest of the demands.

When it became clear that Hitler had no intention of sticking to his side of the bargain, Schuschnigg played his last card. At Berchtesgaden Hitler had dared him to call a referendum on Austrian independence; now the Chancellor decided to call the Führer's bluff. On 9 March he announced in Innsbruck that a plebiscite would be held that coming Sunday, 13 March. The question the government would put to the population was: 'Are you in favour of a free and German, independent and social, a Christian and united Austria?' Most commentators agree that the referendum would have produced a two-thirds 'yes' vote. The fact that the age threshold for voting was set at 24 was very much in the government's favour as it ruled out a substantial chunk of Nazi supporters.

Hitler was well aware of the likely outcome of the plebiscite, which would have been a personal humiliation for him and thrown his plans for German expansion into disarray. He therefore moved fast to wreck Schuschnigg's scheme, and put his generals on alert. An ultimatum was sent to the Austrian Chancellor threatening an invasion if the referendum were not called off immediately. Schuschnigg desperately tried to contact Mussolini for assistance, but the latter was permanently 'unavailable'. (Later it emerged that when Dollfuss's widow addressed a similar plea to the Italian dictator, he merely advised her to flee to Switzerland as quickly as possible.) Abandoned by the country's former friend and protector, and with neither Britain nor France showing the slightest willingness to commit themselves, Schuschnigg caved in. Berlin now demanded the appointment of Arthur Seyss-Inquart, a German nationalist who had been made Minister of the Interior in line with the July agreement, as Chancellor. President Miklas held out for a while longer, but finally complied with Germany's wishes. The new Chancellor was only in the job for two days. Once Hitler had reassurance from Mussolini that Italy would not intervene, the German tanks started rolling in on 12 March 1938 – in response to Seyss-Inquart's 'request' to help restore order – and Austria was annexed to the German Reich.

There were some minor skirmishes on the border, but otherwise the Anschluss proceeded peacefully. Even Hitler was surprised by just how positively the Austrians reacted to the annexation. The jubilant crowds that lined the streets of

Linz, or those that filled Vienna's Heldenplatz to welcome the Führer were genuinely delighted. To be sure, many stayed away from the scenes of celebration, but given that Schuschnigg's plebiscite had expected to result in a comfortable pro-Austria victory, could it be that large swathes of the population had simply turned Nazi overnight? More likely it was the Austrians' schizophrenic attitude towards their identity that enabled such a sudden switch of allegiance. Throughout the inter-war years Austrian patriotism was mostly very weak, and always highly contingent. German national feeling remained strong in Austria, even amongst those highly committed to the Austrian cause (Schuschnigg is a good case in point here). When Anschluss came, supporters of Austrian independence may have felt mixed emotions.

Renner provides us with another fascinating case of this dual identity. His initial reaction to the Anschluss was to flee Austria with his family. To this end he had devised what he thought to be an ingenious plan: he reserved rooms at the Hotel Adlon in Berlin, reckoning that Germany would represent the least suspicious escape route. But aged 67, he felt on reflection too old for emigration and a new start, and so abandoned the plan. Instead, he suddenly and unexpectedly thrust himself into the limelight again by voicing his endorsement for Anschluss. It seems he flirted with the idea of orchestrating a public campaign to support the annexation, but Hitler's deputy, Rudolf Hess, would only consent to Renner giving an interview for the *Neues Wiener Tagblatt* on 3 April 1938. He said the following: *Although not carried out using methods I approve of, the Anschluss has now taken place, it is an historical fact, and I truly see it as compensation for the humiliation of 1918 and 1919, for St Germain and Versailles. I would have to deny the whole of my past as a theoretical campaigner for national self-determination, and as a German-Austrian statesman if I did not gladly welcome this great historical event: the reunification of the German nation.*[9]

This interview has provoked much analysis and given rise to different theories about why Renner was so ready to defend the Nazi takeover. The usual hypothesis rolled out by Renner apologists – and also his wife, Luise – was that he wished to protect some of his party comrades, like the Jewish Robert Danneberg. From his exile Otto Bauer, who died shortly afterwards, assumed that Renner as a high-profile figure had been pressurised or blackmailed into it. But Renner himself insisted afterwards that he had spoken from conviction. In a subsequent interview, this time for the English *World Review*, he explained that he had expressed himself *spontaneously and in complete freedom*, even though he regretted submitting himself to a regime with an incomprehensible racial policy. He concluded this interview with the conviction that *states remain but systems change. I cannot refuse something that I have wished for with all my strength because it has been achieved in another way than mine.*[10]

Immediately after the Second World War Renner tried to distance himself from his earlier comments, and argued that he had wanted to get the Nazis off his back. He also maintained that any other response would have caused unnecessary sacrifices. A certain amount of self-justification here, no doubt, but Renner's excuses do contain an element of truth. Although he was kept under observation during the War, Renner did avoid Gestapo unpleasantness, and moreover his Jewish son-in-law, Hans Deutsch, was given permission to leave the country with the three grandchildren. They moved to Britain with Renner's daughter, although she returned to Austria soon afterwards as she missed her parents.

Renner's German-national sentiments found further expression in an even more extraordinary document from later in 1938. As it was never published, it has frequently been overlooked – or perhaps deliberately ignored – by commentators. This is a brochure which surveys the issue of Greater Germany from the dissolution of the Monarchy to the Nazi acquisition of the Sudetenland. With its doubts as to the effectiveness of parliamentary democracy in Austria, the brochure seems to pervert everything Renner believed in; his criticism of Dollfuss, moreover, is not based on the latter's authoritarian coup, but on his having seduced the Austrians into believing they were a nation unto themselves. He welcomes the incorporation of the Sudeten areas into the Reich, praising the tenacity and spirit of the Nazi leaders for the success of the Munich Agreement. Perhaps even more shockingly, he denounces Wilhelm Miklas and Leopold Kunschak as long-term opponents of Anschluss, and also castigates Otto Ender for his 'treacherous' separatism as Governor of Vorarlberg.

The Anschluss unleashed a passionate campaign of hostility against the Jews of Austria. Anti-Semitism had a long history in this part of the world; indeed the Christian Social Party had begun life in the 19th century as an anti-Semitic coalition of Catholic groupings. It was, however, a religious and economic anti-Semitism, closely connected with anti-liberal ideas, rather than a racial discrimination that dominated until the Nazi takeover. During the First Republic anti-Semitism provided some of the glue that held the Christian Socials and Pan-Germans together. Politicians on the right understood that anti-Jewish propaganda was an indispensable tool for electoral success, as it tapped into a rich seam of resentment in the Austrian consciousness. The *Heimwehr* recognised this, too, and disseminated anti-Semitic propaganda more freely than the bourgeois coalition parties. Despite this, actual instances of violence against Jews were rare in the republican era. The most serious incident was at the 1925 World Zionist Conference in Vienna, as a result of which more than 100 people were arrested and many injured. Even with the advent of Austro-Fascism and the introduction of the corporate constitution which emphasised the Christian-German character of the state, Jews still enjoyed rights of equal citizenship. There were haphazard attempts to segregate Jews in schools in Vienna and the Burgenland, as well as an unsystematic policy of discrimination in the civil service, but the latter was aimed more at Social Democrats than Jews.[11]

When the Nazi takeover – and with it the implementation of the Nuremberg Laws – gave the green light to Jewish persecution, however, the Austrians needed no further encouragement. Jew-baiting and plundering of Jewish property began immediately, while efforts to force Jewish people to emigrate were more zealous and thorough in Austria then in the rest of the Reich. Overall, around two-thirds of Austrian Jews (who numbered in excess of 200,000) emigrated in the years 1938–41, while the remaining third were killed as part of the Final Solution. Austrian Nazis played a full part in the attempted eradication of European Jewry, and the number of Austrians who made up the ranks of the SS was disproportionately high.[12]

Unlike many of his former party colleagues, Renner had a fairly comfortable war; he was one of the few Austrian politicians not to suffer Nazi persecution. The authorities recognised that he had belonged to the right wing of the Social Democratic Party and had never behaved radically. Critics of Renner maintain that he went out of his way to avoid contact with 'illegal' socialist cells during the Nazi occupation; he certainly had nothing to do with the resistance. He remained under constant supervision, however, and the few friends that paid him visits at home had to report to the Gestapo. He was permitted to go to Vienna every Thursday, where he would visit his sister or play cards in various coffee houses, but he was forced (!) to travel first class to avoid coming into contact with the general population.

Most of the time was spent at home, where the Renners' productive vegetable garden allowed them a varied diet by wartime standards. Karl followed a strict routine which saw mornings dedicated to reading, language studies or writing, while the afternoons would be spent in the company of his family, or occasionally friends. He began work on his memoirs – only one volume of which was ever published – as well as a history of Austria since 1918, which did not appear until after his death. Renner also embarked on another major tome, *Weltbild der Moderne*, a verse epic inspired by the natural environment around him. This was also published posthumously.

For some of the leading Austrian Nazis the shine was taken off Anschluss when it emerged that they would not be personally rewarded for their years of struggle against the Austro-Fascist regime. They had hoped they would be able to run an autonomous Austrian unit within the Reich; instead the top jobs were given to 'outsiders' and, in a two-stage process, Austria was stripped of all collective identity and was wholly absorbed into Greater Germany. Disillusionment with the Nazi regime became more widespread as the victories in the first years of the War gave way to stalemates and defeats, bringing ever greater hardship to the population at large. In spite of this, active resistance was only on a small scale, chiefly the efforts of communists and monarchists.

The declared intent of the Dollfuss-Schuschnigg regime had been to rid the country of the divisiveness of party politics and replace this with a unified sense of patriotism. In the event, the 'Austro-Fascist' experiment did not succeed in winning the active support of the population any more than the republican system had; the dictatorship merely widened further the division between left and right that had opened up in the 1920s. The Anschluss that so many had dreamed of was finally realised in March 1938, albeit not in the form that had been once imagined or even desired. But with the much-despised Treaty of St Germain now in shreds, and as part of a Great Power once more, the Austrians were able to experience – if only briefly – a feeling of (German) national pride. Within a few months this would lead the Austrians into barbarity; and within a few years to military defeat yet again.

9

The Rebirth of Austria

In 1943 the Allied Powers issued the Moscow Declaration, which conceded that Austria had been the first victim of Nazi aggression, and expressed their wish to see a free and independent Austria restored after the War. The following clause was also included: 'Austria is reminded, however, that she has a responsibility which she cannot evade for participation in the War on the side of Hitler-Germany, and that in the final settlement account will inevitably be taken of her own contribution to her liberation.'[1] In perpetrating the myth of Austrians as victims, the Allied declaration provided a foundation stone for independent Austrian statehood after the War, and encouraged future political leaders, as well as the wider public, finally to reorient their national consciousness away from Germanness. The adaptable Renner was undergoing this process, too.

The Soviets were the first of the Allied armies to enter Austria at the end of the War, reaching Gloggnitz – from where the National Socialists had already fled – on 1 April 1945. Their arrival spurred Renner straight back into action after a decade on the sidelines. He ordered two socialist functionaries to set up a democratic municipal government, and then established contact with the Soviet military authority. With the help of a Czech foreign worker who spoke patchy Russian, he issued a protest against the brutality shown by the Soviet soldiers towards civilians as they searched houses for hidden weapons; and also tried to organise food supplies for the starving local population. After being passed from officer to officer he was driven to the main headquarters of the 9th Guards Division in Hochwolkersdorf (about 25km from Gloggnitz) where he was received on 5 April by Colonel-General Alexei Zheltov. In addition to voicing his immediate concerns for the welfare of the citizens of Gloggnitz, Renner also offered his services to help re-establish the Republic of Austria.

It was long thought to have been serendipitous that Renner and the Soviet authorities should have 'found' each other in the spring of 1945. More recently it has been shown that the encounter was not so coincidental. We have seen that Renner had a strong sense of mission throughout his life, mixed with a dash of self-importance. After the First World War he believed that he was the man to rebuild Austria from the imperial rubble, and he smartly manoeuvred himself into the twin roles of head of government and head of the peace delegation to Paris. Finding it difficult to stand aside from major political developments, and with a wealth of experience behind him, it is not surprising that he should have asserted himself so forcefully in April 1945.

As far as the Soviets were concerned, meanwhile, Renner was anything but anonymous. He was the only Austrian socialist whose name was known to Stalin – largely due to his writings on the nationality question in the Monarchy – and the Soviet dictator had earmarked Renner for a position of responsibility in Austria when the War was over. It has been widely argued that his advanced age (Renner was now 74) would have picked him out as easy to manipulate, while his public 'yes' to Anschluss in 1938 had so compromised the former Chancellor that he would have seemed likely to be compliant with Russian wishes. Although this hypothesis has been more recently questioned, as it relies on the unproven assumption that Stalin had a fixed plan for a communist take-over in Austria,[2] it is nonetheless clear that Renner's involvement was at the very least an administrative convenience for the Soviet authorities. And they seemed very happy to indulge this grand old man of Austrian socialism. When asked what he might need to help him carry out his difficult duties, Renner went to consult his wife and returned the next day with a long list starting with household items and clothes, and ending with a ham, bay leaves and pepper. Moreover, at the end of one of his meetings with the Russians, he spied a box of Austrian cigars, picked them up, and said with a smile: *The expropriators must be expropriated.*[3]

On 9 April Renner moved with his family from Gloggnitz to Schloss Eichbühl in nearby Wiener Neustadt. There he worked industriously for 12 days on plans for the re-establishment of Austria, favouring a more centralised system, and a return to the 1920 constitution. In this time he wrote Stalin an obsequious letter, thanking the Soviet Union profusely for having liberated his country from the Nazi yoke and calling on the dictator to take Austria under his mighty protection. Renner also stated that he saw it as his *absolute duty* to place himself in the service of rebuilding his country, and listed the many things he thought qualified him for the job. His fawning continued with a pledge that the Social Democrats would work together with the communists to re-found the republic step by step, and his conviction that the future of Austria belonged to socialism.[4] Notwithstanding the *faux pas* whereby Renner proudly mentioned his former contacts with Trotsky, this long missive was a masterly combination of sycophancy and self-promotion. In the medium term it may have done more harm than good; with Stalin's mind already made up, all it did was reinforce the suspicions of the Western Allies that Renner was a Soviet puppet.

When Renner met Marshal Tolbukhin in Vienna on 20 April, he was surprised to learn that three political parties – the Social Democrats, Communist Party and People's Party (former Christian Socials) – had been formed already. The Communists protested against Renner's appointment as Chancellor, but he had Stalin's confidence and set about forming a provisional government. For all the promises he had made to the Soviet leader, Renner only wanted to see token Communist representation in the new cabinet. But the wishes of the Soviet High Command could not be ignored, and Renner conceded the Ministries of the Interior and of Education to the Communist Party. There were two ministries for the People's Party as well, making it a very broad-based government. Most of the cabinet posts were taken by moderate socialists, however, and Renner also appointed two under-secretaries from the other parties to each ministry, thus enabling him to keep a watchful eye over all the departments of his administration, particularly those headed by the Communists.

Although Tolbukhin gave approval to Renner's government on 27 April, London and Washington failed to recognise this *fait accompli*. Besides the concern that Renner was a pawn in the hands of the Soviets – which was only heightened by the appointment of a Communist as Minister of the

Interior – the British protested that no Allied Commission had yet been established in Austria. What is more, fighting was still continuing in other parts of the country, and the state infrastructure was in tatters. Postal and radio services were not functioning, while the government had no trains and only two cars at its disposal. Keeping order presented the government with a major challenge. Typhoid and dysentery raged through Vienna, yet the sanitary system was a wreck, there were no ambulances, and there was a massive shortage of doctors and medicines. Homes were also being looted by criminals, and cases of women being raped were not uncommon.

When the cabinet first met on 30 April, Renner was fairly autocratic in his approach to government business. Ernst Fischer, the Communist Minister of Education, called Renner's style of government a 'presidential dictatorship'.[5] When the Communists complained about the provisional constitution, the Chancellor threatened his resignation, and this was sufficient to shut them up. Even Karl Seitz, recently returned from Ravensbrück concentration camp, was critical of Renner's authoritarian manner.[6] In his determination to banish the spectre of the inter-war political strife that had crippled Austria, Renner aimed to be a Chancellor above the parties. To the chagrin of his colleagues, he stopped attending Social Democratic Party meetings.

At the Potsdam Conference of August 1945, Britain and America still refused to recognise the Renner government, which meant that its authority only extended to the limits of the Soviet zone. The western provinces of Austria, under the control of the other Allies, were prevented from establishing political contact with Renner's regime. It was not until the middle of September 1945, after the Western Allies had taken up their posts in Vienna, that the whole of Austria officially came under Four-Power rule: Soviet, American, British and French. When Renner expanded his cabinet to include representatives of the western provinces – thereby increasing the influence of the People's Party in government – and announced a general election for November, the doubts of the Western Allies were overcome. The Chancellor's authority was now nationwide.

The election was a triumph for the two main parties. With around 800,000 former members of the Nazi Party prohibited from voting, the People's Party won 85 seats, the Social Democrats 76 seats, while the communists made a miserable showing, winning only 5 per cent of the votes and four seats. Leopold Figl, who had been a minor player in the Austro-Fascist regime, became Chancellor and headed a grand coalition of the two main parties, which included a token Communist as Minister for Electrification and Energy. But Renner was not finished yet. Six days after his 75th birthday – which had been celebrated by a party for 2,000 people in the Wiener Konzerthaus – he was unanimously elected first President of the Second Republic by the combined assembly of the two Parliamentary chambers.

Back in the 1920s, when the Christian Socials had sought to establish a more authoritarian system of government in Austria, Renner opposed the moves to weaken the sovereignty of Parliament in favour of a strong presidential figure. Now that he had acceded to this esteemed position himself, Renner was keen to extract as much from the Presidency as possible, rather than settling for a back-seat, ceremonial role. He started by upgrading the presidential offices – which had formerly consisted of a few rooms within the Chancellery – and moved to Maria Theresia's suite in the Hofburg (the

Habsburgs' winter palace in the centre of Vienna). Those on the left of the Social Democratic Party thought he had become more conservative since his appointment as President, but this apparent drift was a natural consequence of his resolve to be a non-partisan head of state. At a People's Party event during the 1949 election campaign, he told a roomful of conservatives, *I have two children: my socialist party and you.*[7] To the nation at large, he came across as a friendly but authoritative grandfatherly figure, his large white beard perhaps providing a subconscious link in Austrian minds with Emperor Franz Joseph.[8]

With the re-establishment of Austria as a political entity, two major problems faced the new republic. The first, and more immediate of the two, was how to start piecing together the country's shattered economy. At the most basic level this meant providing enough food for a starving population. The official food ration in Vienna dropped to 600 calories per day at one point, lower even than concentration camp levels. In May Renner sent Stalin a note explaining that there were only three weeks of food supplies left, although it was ten weeks until the next harvest. Stalin responded with immediate assistance, using supplies that had been captured from the German army. The 1945 harvest was a poor one, however, and the winter that followed particularly harsh. American flour reserves helped push the ration up to 1,550 calories during the winter months, only for it to be cut back down to 1,200 when spring arrived.[9] The problem of feeding the population was compounded by a flood of 'German' refugees from Prague, Brno and southern Moravia, around 300,000 in all, who were driven out by a Czech population hell-bent on revenge for the crimes of 1938–45. The introduction of the Marshall Plan into Austria in 1947 soon relieved the food crisis, and rationing for bread and flour was abolished early in 1949. By the same time the shoots of economic recovery were also visible: the currency had stabilised and industrial production had surpassed pre-war levels.

The other, more long-term problem was how to bring about a rapid end to the four-power occupation and thus achieve full sovereignty. However grateful the Austrian people were for their liberation in 1945, and for the material assistance the Allies gave them, a feeling gradually developed that one foreign occupation had merely been replaced by another. Naively, Renner had assumed that Austria would be in a position to agree a State Treaty with the Allies within a few months of the end of hostilities. The initial discord between the Soviet Union and the Western Allies over the legitimacy of the Renner administration was only a foretaste of a much wider hostility between the two sides. Like Germany, Austria was caught between East and West, and as the Cold War set in, the very real possibility existed that it might end up divided into two states. The four-power occupation had already created separate economic areas; the Western Zones were trading with Switzerland, Germany and Italy prior to the re-establishment of a functioning Austrian internal market. On the other hand, a political concession by the Soviets in June 1946 meant that, from now on, all Austrian laws passed by Parliament would come into effect unless the Control Council unanimously rejected them. With the abolition of the Soviet veto, the Austrian government gained more control over its own affairs.

As the full horror of the crimes committed under the Third Reich was revealed, it became politically expedient for Austria to distance itself from Germany as much as possible. The Moscow Declaration of 1943 had created the victim myth, which the post-war leaders eagerly seized hold of to underpin a new construct of Austrian identity. Gone was the close association with the German nation and German culture, and in came a formula which took as its reference point the Western theory of the nation as a political rather than ethnic construct. It took a long time for this clean break with Germany to filter down into the consciousness of the Austrian people as a whole. In 1965, a survey showed that only 48 per cent agreed with the proposition that Austria was a nation; by 1980 this figure had risen to 67 per cent.[10]

Any new identity involves a certain amount of rewriting the past. In the case of post-war Austria this meant focusing on the first part of the Moscow Declaration; on 27 April 1945, Renner's coalition government declared the Anschluss, executed by military occupation, to be null and void. Austria, the statement continued, had been the first victim of Hitler's aggressive foreign policy. In 1946 the Foreign Ministry issued a publication entitled *Rot-Weiss-Rot-Buch* (Red-White-Red Book, after the colours of the Austrian flag), containing a selection of documents from the period 1933–45 relating specifically to Austria's role before and during Anschluss, as well as the events of the Second World War. Amongst other omissions, it failed to mention Renner's affirmation of the Anschluss, and although the book admitted that some Austrians had been opportunistic in 1938, the official conclusion ran: 'The Austrian people did not, however, go over to National Socialism, even then. Anybody who knows the Austrians even a little, will understand that Prussianism, militarism and National Socialism are basically as alien and abhorrent to them as to any other people in Europe. The military cult of Prussia, the totalitarian idea and the complete domination of the individual by the state have always been, and still are, diametrically opposed to the Austrian character.'[11]

The second half of the Moscow Declaration, which drew attention to Austria's participation in the War on the side of Nazi Germany, was quietly forgotten and eventually removed from the preamble to the 1955 State Treaty. To be fair, denazification procedures were established as in Germany, although a major difference here was that the Austrian authorities were left to manage the process themselves, whereas in Germany it was the Allies who executed the policy in their respective zones. Action against minor offenders, who amounted to about 90 per cent of all those under investigation, was soon abandoned however, and former Austrian Nazis were welcomed back into the political fold and given the vote in the 1949 election. What is more, denazification was not accompanied by a parallel process of re-education, and so a collective amnesia about the past quickly took hold. Take Renner's comment from 1946 in which he doubted, given the current mood of the country, that *Austria ... would again allow Jews to build up a family monopoly. Of course we would not allow a new Jewish community from eastern Europe to come over here and establish themselves while our own people need work.*[12] It is inconceivable that a comparable German statesman, such as Adenauer, would have ever uttered such words. Renner's observation not only reveals a blind spot he personally had *vis-à-vis* the atrocities committed against Jews under the Nazi regime during the Third Reich, but also reflects a nationwide tendency, bolstered by the victim myth, to deny complicity in the crimes of the Third Reich. It was easy enough to shift all the blame to Berlin.

When Renner turned 80 on 14 December 1950, an outsider would have been forgiven for thinking that Vienna had wound the clock back 40 years to recreate Franz Joseph's 80th birthday. At a special sitting of Parliament, the President was greeted by a fanfare as if he were the Emperor himself. Only the Communist members of the Nationalrat – all five of them – refused to participate in this theatrical gesture. The entire country celebrated his birthday; festivities were held everywhere. Two days previously he had been made an honorary citizen of Vienna; now he was the guest of honour at a succession of parties. It may be that the endless socialising took its toll; on 24 December he suffered a stroke and never regained consciousness. Karl Renner died in Vienna on New Year's Eve 1950.

Renner departed this life at the height of his esteem. He had become a myth, a symbol of the new Austria; as a public figure he had achieved the status of 'untouchable'. He never lived to witness the signing of the State Treaty by which Austria regained full independence. For him, the endless delay in settling the Austrian question was something of a personal affront, as he felt the Western Allies had never paid him sufficient respect in the months immediately following the liberation of Vienna. Nonetheless, he would have been delighted to see the smooth re-establishment of parliamentary democracy, and specifically the advent of consensus politics in Austria after the bitter antagonism of the inter-war years. So great was the consensus, in fact, that the two main parties (the Communists dropped out in 1947) remained in coalition until 1966. A striking, peculiarly Austrian manifestation of this accommodation was the *Proporz* system, whereby posts in the public sector were allocated proportionately to supporters of the two parties, based on their relative strength in Parliament. The downside of this cosy arrangement was a stagnation of political life and the inevitable spectre of corruption.

The political stability of the post-war years which had

evaded the First Republic was mirrored by rapid and sustained economic growth that propelled Austria to become one of the richest countries in the world. In short, the country became a prosperous, secure place to live, seemingly happy with its newly-fashioned identity as an independent, neutral nation at the heart of Europe, and generally getting on with things quietly. Happy to cash in on its glorious imperial past, breathtaking landscapes and ideal location for winter sports, Austria attracted tourists by the millions, but otherwise was a relatively silent bit-player on the international stage. Yet two headline-grabbing controversies would thrust the country into the global spotlight once more, and cause it to re-evaluate its new identify and recent history.

On 15 May 1955 the Austrian State Treaty was concluded at the Belvedere Palace in Vienna. Signing for Austria was the Christian Social Foreign Minister, Leopold Figl. Based on the 1943 Moscow Declaration, the treaty restored full sovereignty to the Republic, which meant the Allies left Austrian soil in October that year. At the same time, the Austrian Parliament made a declaration of permanent neutrality, which satisfied the Soviet desire to prevent the country from joining NATO. Austria became a member of the EU in 1995.

The first of these erupted in 1986, when former Secretary-General of the United Nations, Kurt Waldheim, was elected President of Austria in spite of disclosures about his time as a *Wehrmacht* intelligence officer in occupied Greece. Although no proof was found of Waldheim's involvement in wartime atrocities, the case prised open the lid on Austria's role in the Third Reich. It finally led to Chancellor Franz Vranitzky's admission in 1991 that the country had not merely been the first victim of Nazi aggression, but that it had a share of responsibility for the War and the crimes of the Third Reich.

The second controversy was the rise in popularity, and ultimate participation in government of the far right in Austria under its charismatic leader, the late Jörg Haider. The astonishing and rapid success of Haider's party (and its offshoot) since the early 1990s has partly been a reaction against the *Proporz* system which Renner's consensus politics helped to establish in the immediate post-war era. It has also been a product of the country's failure to face the truth behind the 1938–45 period. For this, the Austrian political leaders of the immediate post-war period, Renner among them, must share some of the responsibility.

Conclusion

The new Republic of Austria was shattered both materially and psychologically by the terms of the Treaty of St Germain. With the dissolution of the 500-year-old Habsburg Monarchy, 'Austria' as it had been understood by the Emperor's subjects disappeared for good. The rump state that Renner and his delegation represented in St Germain was a grouping of German Alpine and Danubian provinces with no collective identity or economic coherence.

This lack of identification with St Germain Austria is highlighted by the endless talk of alternative solutions, whether they were Anschluss, Danube federation or individual provinces going their own way. What nobody seemed prepared to accept was that an independent Austrian state was anything more than a provisional entity. All it needed was a change in the international climate for Austria to be freed from the prison of the Peace Treaty. This came about following Hitler's rise to power in Germany and the growing awareness that the Versailles signatories were not going to stand by its terms if that meant entering into another war. Anschluss was now a real possibility, but did the Austrians still want it?

Competing narratives of Austrian patriotism – bound

up heavily with the imperial past and containing a strong element of anti-Prussianism – and German national feeling made for potential confusion in the allegiance of the Austrians. It was, in fact, possible to harbour loyalty to both, as was shown by Renner and many of the leading politicians on the right. The balance was upset, however, by the introduction of Nazi propaganda into the general discourse, which promoted a modern, dynamic and racial form of German nationalism. In theory this ideology was anathema to both Catholic conservatives and socialists in Austria; in practice it won over a significant proportion of the population who believed it might achieve more for them than had either a failed parliamentary democracy or the semi-imported fascism of Dollfuss' corporate state. The Anschluss of 1938 may not have been quite what the supporters of union had envisaged after the First World War, but it represented a change, a liberation from the diktat of St Germain.

After the Second World War, Austrian leaders were quick to learn from the political mistakes of the First Republic, promoting both political consensus and a national identity based on the Western European model. Assisted by an economic miracle that drove long-term growth, and a widespread desire to paper over the past (which the Allies allowed to happen), it was possible to forge an identification with an independent Austrian state that had simply not been feasible in the wake of the Paris Peace Conference.

Karl Renner, the founding father of both the First and Second Republics, could claim to have been the second most important Austrian politician of the 20th century after Adolf Hitler. Born into a farming family which fell into severe poverty, he grew up with an urge to achieve practical change for the economically disadvantaged, which was reinforced by his contact as a student with the industrial proletariat in Vienna. Although Marxism informed his theoretical writings, as a politician he was highly pragmatic and flexible. This set him at odds with the dominant left wing of his party in the First Republic, who preferred to remain true to their ideology rather than sully it through concessions to their conservative political opponents. At every turn Renner seemed willing to compromise – even when this ran counter to his principles – although the hostile political climate of the inter-war years did not provide fertile ground for his brand of *Realpolitik*. It was after the Second World War that Renner's style of politics came into its own and paved the way for the consensus of coalition government. The mythical figure that Renner had become by the time of his death in December 1950 was largely symbolic of how the Austrians wished to see themselves and be seen by others. He symbolised in person the arduous journey the Austrians had made from empire through to post-war reconstruction, via St Germain, civil war and Nazi occupation. His story chimed with the 'official' narrative of this journey (which conveniently left out the uncomfortable bits) and he ultimately emerged a survivor with a smile on his face.

> 'Our people possesses such a marked individuality, different from all other peoples, that it ... [can] pronounce itself an independent nation. Its tie to the Germans of the Reich by a common language can be no obstacle.'
> **RENNER, OCTOBER 1946[1]**

When the myth of Austria's victimhood started to unravel in the wake of Waldheim and Haider, it was thus only natural that the Renner myth should be subjected to revision, too. The skilful politician became the unprincipled opportunist; the great paternal figure of the nation became the creep who had cosied up to the Führer by publicising his support for the Anschluss. There is no doubt that some of the less appealing aspects of his life had been suppressed, including by Renner himself, but in some quarters the utterances and writings from 1938 started to overshadow all else, as if they alone painted a true picture of the man.[2]

But even if we strip away the myth of Renner to reveal all his weaknesses and failings, we are still left with an impressive list of achievements: his mammoth efforts, often overlooked, for the co-operative movement throughout his life; his tireless and good-humoured endeavours against the odds at St Germain; his contribution to the 1920 constitution; the far-reaching social reforms of his first government; his interventions to produce a compromise on the 1929 constitution; the neutering of the Austrian Communists in the early months following the liberation of Vienna; his adept handling of the Soviets; his skilful reuniting of the country after 1945; the establishment of consensus politics; not to mention a vast scholarly and literary output. Renner wore his public face with ease, exuded charm and enjoyed the political limelight. At the same time, however, he was essentially a private man, who preferred the company of his immediate family and a handful of close friends. For those outside this circle, he was difficult to get to know intimately,[3] which is perhaps why – with his apparent inconsistencies, contradictions and U-turns – the real Karl Renner has remained a somewhat fugitive figure.

Notes

Preface: 'A Man for All Seasons'

1. Details of the signing have been taken from *The Times*, 11 September 1919, p 10, and *New York Times*, 11 September 1919, p 12.

2. See Anton Pelinka, 'Karl Renner – A Man for All Seasons' in *Austrian History Yearbook*, Vol XXIII (1992) pp 111–19.

1 The Multinational Empire

1. Viktor von Andrian-Werburg, cited in Robert A Kann, *The Multinational Empire: Nationalism and National Reform in the Habsburg Monarchy 1848–1918. Volume I: Empire and Nationalities* (Octagon Books, New York: 1977) p 3.

2. C A Macartney, *The Habsburg Empire 1790–1918* (Weidenfeld and Nicholson, London: 1968) p 548.

3. Karl Renner, *An der Wende zweier Zeiten: Lebenserinnerungen von Karl Renner, Vol I* (Danubia Verlag, Vienna: 1946) p 15, hereafter *Lebenserinnerungen*. Most of the biographical

information about Renner's childhood comes from this
memoir and therefore ought to be treated with a certain
caution.

4. *Lebenserinnerungen*, pp 93–4.
5. *Lebenserinnerungen*, p 139.
6. Walter Rauscher, *Karl Renner: Ein österreichischer Mythos* (Ueberreuter, Vienna: 1995) p 25, hereafter Rauscher.

2 National Conflict

1. A wealth of comparative figures are reproduced in Paul Kennedy, *The Rise and Fall of the Great Powers* (Vintage, New York: 1989).
2. *Lebenserinnerungen*, pp 219–21.
3. *Lebenserinnerungen*, pp 235–6.
4. Mark Twain, 'Stirring Times in Austria' in *Harper's Magazine* (March 1898) pp 530–40.
5. See Karl Renner, 'State and Nation' (trans Joseph O'Donnell) in Ephraim Nimni (ed), *National Cultural Autonomy and its Contemporary Critics* (Routledge, London and New York: 2005) pp 15–47.

3 Twilight of the Empire

1. Rauscher, pp 68–70.
2. Siegfried Nasko and Johannes Reichl (eds), *Karl Renner: Zwischen Anschluß und Europa* (Verlag Holzhausen, Vienna: 2000) p 30, hereafter Nasko and Reichl.
3. Rauscher, p 88.
4. Manfred Rauchensteiner, 'Austria in the First World War, 1914–1918' in Rolf Steiniger, Günter Bischof and Michael Gehler (eds), *Austria in the Twentieth Century*

(Transaction Publishers, New Brunswick and London: 2002) p 41.

5. Rauscher, p 90.
6. Nasko and Reichl, p 32.
7. Nasko and Reichl, pp 35–9.

4 Prelude to the Treaty

1. Harold Nicolson, *Peacemaking 1919* (Methuen, London: 1964) p 293.
2. F L Carsten, *The First Austrian Republic 1918–1938. A Study Based on British and Austrian Documents* (Gower, Cambridge: 1986) p 14, hereafter Carsten.
3. Carsten, p 14.
4. Alfred Low, *The Anschluss Movement 1918–1919 and the Paris Peace Conference* (American Philosophical Society, Philadelphia: 1974) p 62, hereafter Low, *1918–1919*.
5. Low, *1918–1919*, pp 51–2.
6. Carsten, p 6.
7. For a summary of the instructions to the Austrian delegation see Low, *1918–1919*, pp 399–401.
8. *Neue Freie Presse*, 8 May 1919, p 1.
9. *Reichspost*, 8 May 1919, p 1.
10. *Neue Freie Presse*, 13 May 1919, p 1.
11. Fritz Fellner (ed), *Saint-Germain im Sommer 1919: Die Briefe Franz Kleins aus der Zeit seiner Mitwirkung in der österreichischen Friedensdelgation. Mai–August 1919, Quellen zur Geschichte des 19. und 20. Jahrhunderts, Band 1* (Verlag Wolfgang Neugebauer, Salzburg: 1977) p 51, hereafter Fellner (ed), *Die Briefe Franz Kleins*.
12. *The Times*, 15 May 1919, p 13.

13. *The Times*, 16 May 1919, p 12.

14. Rauscher, p 164.

15. *The Times*, 15 May 1919, p 13.

16. Fellner (ed), *Die Briefe Franz Kleins*, p 55.

17. Fellner (ed), *Die Briefe Franz Kleins*, p 68.

18. Nasko and Reichl, p 212.

19. Nasko and Reichl, p 259.

20. Fellner (ed), *Die Briefe Franz Kleins*, pp 52, 99–100.

21. Fellner (ed), *Die Briefe Franz Kleins*, p 100.

22. Fellner (ed), *Die Briefe Franz Kleins*, p 106.

23. Margaret MacMillan, *Peacemakers: The Paris Conference of 1919 and Its Attempt to End War* (John Murray, London: 2001) p 260.

24. Fellner (ed), *Die Briefe Franz Kleins*, p 93.

25. Fellner (ed), *Die Briefe Franz Kleins*, pp 102–3.

5 The Treaty of St Germain

1. *The Times*, 3 June 1919, p 13.

2. A detailed summary of the draft treaty can be found in *The Times*, 3 June 1919, p 14.

3. *The Times*, 3 June 1919, p 13.

4. MacMillan, *Peacemakers*, p 261.

5. MacMillan, *Peacemakers*, p 261.

6. Fellner (ed), *Die Briefe Franz Kleins*, pp 106–7.

7. Nasko and Reichl, p 260.

8. Fellner (ed), *Die Briefe Franz Kleins*, p 116.

9. For an English text of Renner's speech see *The Times*, 3 June 1919, p 11.

10. *The Times*, 3 June 1919, p 11.

11. *The Times*, 5 June 1919, p 16.

12. Nasko and Reichl, p 262.

13. See Rauscher, p 170.

14. *The Times*, 7 June 1919, p 11.

15. Low, *1918–1919*, pp 414–15.

16. This digest of press reaction in Austria appears in *The Times*, 7 June 1919, p 11.

17. Cited in Nasko and Reichl, p 262.

18. Fellner (ed), *Die Briefe Franz Kleins*, p 143.

19. *The Times*, 12 June 1919, p 14.

20. Otto Ender, *Vorarlbergs Schweizer-Anschluß-Bewegung von 1918 bis 1924: Schriften zur Vorarlberger Landeskunde Band 5* (Vorarlberger Verlagsanstalt, Dornbin: 1952) p 10.

21. *The Times*, 10 July 1919, p 11.

22. *The Times*, 9 July 1919, p 11.

23. Nasko and Reichl, p 263.

24. Fellner (ed), *Die Briefe Franz Kleins*, pp 143, 150.

25. Fellner (ed), *Die Briefe Franz Kleins*, pp 165–6.

26. Fellner (ed), *Die Briefe Franz Kleins*, pp 173, 177.

27. Fellner (ed), *Die Briefe Franz Kleins*, p 194.

28. Fellner (ed), *Die Briefe Franz Kleins*, p 194.

29. Nasko and Reichl, p 264.

30. Siegfried Nasko (ed), *Karl Renner in Dokumenten und Erinnerungen* (Österreichischer Bundesverlag, Vienna: 1982) p 64.

31. Fellner (ed), *Die Briefe Franz Kleins*, p 246.

32. Low, *1918–1919*, pp 424–9.

33. For more details see *The Times*, 21 July 1919, p 10.

34. *The Times*, 21 July 1919, p 10.

35. Fellner (ed), *Die Briefe Franz Kleins*, pp 264–5.

36. *Reichspost*, 22 July 1919, p 1.

37. *Neue Freie Presse*, 22 July 1919, p 2.

38. *The Times*, 26 July 1919, p 11.

39. Nasko and Reichl, p 265.

40. Low, *1918–1919*, p 436.
41. The text of the letter, which details all the Treaty revisions, is reproduced in *The Times*, 3 September 1919, pp 10, 12.
42. Low, *1918–1919*, p 439.
43. *New York Times*, 11 September 1919, p 12.
44. *New York Times*, 11 September 1919, p 12.
45. Nasko and Reichl, pp 267–8.

6 The State that No-one Wanted

1. This is the title of a history of the First Republic by Hellmut Andics.
2. See Alfred Low, *The Anschluss Movement, 1931–1938, and the Great Powers* (East European Monographs, Boulder: 1985) pp 28–9, hereafter Low, *1931–1938*.
3. *The Times*, 21 November 1919, p 11.
4. *The Times*, 8 December 1919, p 13.
5. *The Times*, 13 December 1919, p 13.
6. *The Times*, 13 December 1919, p 13.
7. *The Times*, 17 December 1919, p 14.
8. Rauscher, p 215.
9. Rauscher, pp 198–9.
10. For more detail on these reforms, see Anton Hoffmann-Ostenhof, 'Social Policy in the Republic of Austria', *Annals of the American Academy of Political and Social Science*, Vol 98 (Nov 1921), Supplement: 'Present Day Social and Industrial Conditions in Austria', pp 56–61.
11. *Neue Freie Presse*, 15 June 1920, p 1.
12. *Reichspost*, 8 July 1920, p 1.
13. Ignaz Seipel, *Nation und Staat* (KK Universitäts-Verlagsbuchhandlung, Vienna and Leipzig: 1916).

14. Walter Goldinger, 'Der geschichtliche Ablauf der Ereignisse in Österreich von 1918 bis 1945' in Heinrich Benedikt (ed), *Geschichte der Republik Österreich* (Verlag für Geschichte und Politik, Vienna: 1954) p 126; Gottlieb Ladner, *Seipel als Überwinder der Staatskrise von Sommer 1922. Zur Geschichte der Entstehung der Genfer Protokolle vom 4. Oktober 1922*, Publikationen des Österreichischen Instituts für Zeitgeschichte Band 1 (Stiasmy Verlag, Vienna and Graz: 1964) p 43, hereafter Ladner.

15. Low, *1931–1938*, p 21.

16. Carsten, p 54.

17. Rauscher, p 237.

18. Carsten, p 43.

19. Rauscher, p 237.

20. Cited in Ladner, pp 9–10.

7 Political Schism

1. Rauscher, p 241.

2. Nasko and Reichl, pp 184–6.

3. Nasko and Reichl, p 179.

4. Nasko and Reichl, pp 180, 191.

5. Nasko and Reichl, p 218.

6. Rauscher, p 244.

7. Carsten, p 100.

8. Rauscher, p 245.

9. Rauscher, p 249.

10. Rauscher, p 252.

11. Carsten, p 121. The Catholic *Reichspost*, however, was in no doubt that the *Schutzbund* itself was to blame for the killings. See *Reichspost*, 15 July 1927, p 1.

12. George Gedye, *Fallen Bastions: The Central European Tragedy* (Victor Gollancz, London: 1939) p 30, hereafter Gedye.
13. Gedye, p 31.
14. Gordon Brook-Shepherd, *The Austrians: A Thousand-Year Odyssey* (Harper Collins, London: 1996) p 261, hereafter Brook-Shepherd.
15. C Earl Edmondson, *The Heimwehr and Austrian Politics 1918–1936* (University of Georgia Press, Athens: 1978) pp 28–9, hereafter Edmondson.
16. Edmondson, p 45.
17. Melanie Sully, *Continuity and Change in Austrian Socialism: The Eternal Quest for the Third Way* (East European Monographs, Boulder: 1982) p 58.
18. Rauscher, p 264.
19. Rauscher, p 269.
20. Rauscher, p 276.

8 Democracy Eclipsed

1. Nasko and Reichl, p 47.
2. Nasko and Reichl, p 47.
3. Gedye, p 123.
4. Rauscher, p 292.
5. Nasko and Reichl, p 214.
6. Rauscher, p 294.
7. Gedye, p 195.
8. Carsten, p 231.
9. Cited in Rauscher, p 297.
10. *World Review*, Vol 5, No 3 (May 1938) pp 22–7.
11. For more on anti-Semitism in Austria, see Peter Pulzer, *The Rise of Political Anti-Semitism in Germany and Austria* (Peter Halban, London: 1988).

12. Radomír Luža, *Austro-German Relations in the Anschluss Era* (Princeton University Press, Princeton and London: 1975) pp 223–7.

9 The Rebirth of Austria
1. *The Times*, 2 November 1943, p 3.
2. Roger Knight, 'The Renner state government and Austrian sovereignty' in Kurt Richard Luther and Peter Pulzer (eds), *Austria 1945–95: Fifty Years of the Second Republic* (Ashgate, Aldershot: 1998) pp 30–1.
3. Nasko and Reichl, p 216.
4. See Brook-Shepherd, pp 378–9.
5. Rauscher, p 324.
6. Rauscher, p 330.
7. Rauscher, p 386.
8. Nasko and Reichl, p 190.
9. Brook-Shepherd, p 386.
10. Felix Kreissler, *Der Österreicher und seine Nation: Ein Lernprozeß mit Hindernissen* (Hermann Böhlaus Nachf., Vienna, Cologne and Graz: 1984) p 496.
11. Anton Pelinka, 'Perception of the Anschluss after 1945' in William E Wright (ed), *Austria, 1938–1988: Anschluss and Fifty Years* (Ariadne Press, Riverside CA: 1995) p 226.
12. Rauscher, p 368.

Conclusion
1. Rauscher, p 369.
2. Nasko and Reichl, p 75.
3. This was the view of his Social Democrat colleague and Austrian President (1957–65) Adolf Schärf. See Siegfried Nasko (ed), *Karl Renner in Dokumenten und*

Erinnerungen (Österreichischer Bundesverlag, Vienna:
1982) p 13.

Chronology

YEAR	AGE	THE LIFE AND THE LAND
1867		Creation of the Dual Monarchy of Austria-Hungary.
1870		14 Dec: Karl Renner is born.
1873	3	Stock market crash in Austria-Hungary.
1878	8	Congress of Berlin: Bosnia and Herzegovina become Habsburg protectorates.
1879	9	Dual Alliance formed between Germany and Austria-Hungary.
1885	15	Renner family forced to sell their home.
1889	19	Social Democratic Party formed.
1890	20	Renner begins studying law in Vienna.
1891	21	16 Aug: Renner's daughter Leopoldine is born. Triple Alliance (Austria-Hungary, Germany, Italy) renewed for 12 years.

YEAR	HISTORY	CULTURE
1867	North German Confederation founded.	Émile Zola, *Thérèse Raquin*.
1870	Franco-Prussian War: Napoleon III defeated at Sedan.	Jules Verne, *Twenty Thousand Leagues Under the Sea*.
1873	Germans withdraw last troops from France.	Leo Tolstoy, *Anna Karenina*.
1878	Russo-Turkish War ends. Electric street lighting introduced in London.	Thomas Hardy, *The Return of the Native*.
1879	Zulu War. Alsace-Lorraine declared integral part of Germany.	Peter Tchaikovsky, *Eugene Onegin*.
1885	Germany annexes Tanganyika and Zanzibar.	W S Gilbert and Arthur Sullivan, *The Mikado*.
1889	Austro-Hungarian Crown Prince Rudolf commits suicide at Mayerling.	Jerome K Jerome, *Three Men in a Boat*.
1890	Germany's Kaiser Wilhelm II dismisses Otto von Bismarck .	Oscar Wilde, *The Picture of Dorian Gray*.
1891	German Kaiser Wilhelm II visits London. Franco-Russian entente. Young Turk Movement founded in Vienna.	Thomas Hardy, *Tess of the D'Urbervilles*. Gustav Mahler, *Symphony No 1*.

YEAR	AGE	THE LIFE AND THE LAND
1897	27	Renner marries Luise Stoicsics.
		Badeni language ordinances for Bohemia cause rioting amongst Germans.
1898	28	Renner awarded his law doctorate.
1899	29	Renner publishes his work *Staat und Nation* on the nationality problem in Austria.
1905	35	Universal male suffrage introduced in Austria.
1907	37	May: Renner wins a seat at Austrian general election.
1908	38	Renner elected to Lower Austrian diet.
		Austria-Hungary formally annexes Bosnia and Herzegovina.
1910	40	Renner buys the villa in Gloggnitz.
1914	44	28 June: Archduke Franz Ferdinand assassinated in Sarajevo.
		28 July: Austria-Hungary declares war on Serbia, starting the First World War.

YEAR	HISTORY	CULTURE
1897	Queen Victoria's Diamond Jubilee. Crete proclaims union with Greece: Ottoman Empire declares war, defeated in Thessaly; Peace of Constantinople.	H G Wells, *The Invisible Man.* Edmond Rostand, *Cyrano de Bergerac.*
1898	Germany's Otto von Bismarck dies.	Henry James, *The Turn of the Screw.*
1899	Second Boer War begins: British defeats at Stormberg, Magersfontein and Colenso ('Black Week').	Rudyard Kipling, *Stalky and Co.* Edward Elgar, *Enigma Variations.*
1905	'Bloody Sunday': police fire on demonstration in St Petersburg.	E M Forster, *Where Angels Fear to Tread.*
1907	Peace Conference held in The Hague.	Joseph Conrad, *The Secret Agent.*
1908	Britain's Edward VII and Russia's Tsar Nicholas II meet at Reval. Ferdinand I declares Bulgaria's independence, assumes title of Tsar.	Kenneth Grahame, *The Wind in the Willows.* Bela Bartok, *String Quartet NO.1.*
1910	Britain's King Edward VII dies; succeeded by George V.	Karl May, *Winnetou.*
1914	First World War: Battles of Mons, the Marne and First Ypres; trench warfare on Western Front; Russians defeated in Battles of Tannenberg and Masurian Lakes.	James Joyce, *Dubliners.* Gustav Holst, *The Planets.* Film: Charlie Chaplin in *Making a Living.*

YEAR	AGE	THE LIFE AND THE LAND
1916	46	21 Oct: Austrian Minister President Count Stürgkh assassinated in Vienna by Friedrich Adler.
		Renner takes job in war provisioning office.
		21 Nov: Emperor Franz Joseph dies aged 86.
1917	47	Mar: Emperor Karl sounds out possibility of separate peace with the Allies – the 'Sixtus Letter'.
1918	48	12 Apr: 'Sixtus Letter' leaked by Clemenceau.
		16 Oct: The Emperor issues manifesto for Austria giving complete autonomy to the nationalities.
		21 Oct: German deputies of the Reichsrat form the Provisional National Assembly for German-Austria.
		3 Nov: Austria-Hungary signs armistice with the Allies.
		12 Nov: Proclamation of German-Austrian Republic in Vienna – Renner becomes Chancellor.

YEAR	HISTORY	CULTURE
1916	First World War: Battles of Verdun, the Somme and Jutland. US President Woodrow Wilson issues Peace Note to belligerents in European war. David Lloyd George becomes British Prime Minister.	Vicente Blasco Ibanez, *The Four Horsemen of the Apocalypse*. Film: *Intolerance*.
1917	First World War: USA declares war on Germany. February Revolution in Russia. German and Russian armistice.	P G Wodehouse, *The Man With Two Left Feet*. T S Eliot, *Prufrock and Other Observations*. Film: *Easy Street*.
1918	First World War: Peace Treaty of Brest-Litovsk signed between Russia and Central Powers; German Spring offensives on Western Front fail; Romania signs Peace of Bucharest with Germany and Austria-Hungary; Allied offensives on Western Front have German army in full retreat; Armistice signed between Allies and Germany. Ex-Tsar Nicholas II and family executed. Kaiser Wilhelm II of Germany abdicates.	Alexander Blok, *The Twelve*. Gerald Manley Hopkins, *Poems*. Luigi Pirandello, *Six Characters in Search of an Author*. Edvard Munch, *Bathing Man*.

YEAR	AGE	THE LIFE AND THE LAND
1919	49	Feb: First elections held in post-imperial Austria.
		2 Mar: Protocol signed, laying the groundwork for Austria's union with Germany.
		15 May: Austrian peace delegation arrives in Paris.
		2 Jun: First draft of St Germain Treaty handed to Austrians.
		15 Jun: Communist putsch attempt in Vienna.
		20 Jul: Second draft of Treaty handed over.
		26 Jul: Renner replaces Bauer as Foreign Minister.
		10 Sep: Renner signs Treaty of St Germain.
1920	50	Mar: League of Nations conference on 'Austrian problem'.
		10 Jun: Social Democrat–Christian Social coalition collapses – Renner resigns as Chancellor.
		1 Oct: Federal constitution for Austria comes into force.
		Plebiscite held in Carinthia.
		15 Dec: Austria joins League of Nations.
1921	51	Apr–May: Tyrol and Salzburg hold plebiscites on unilateral Anschluss with Germany.
1922	52	4 Oct: Seipel signs Geneva Protocols.
1923	53	1 Jan: Workers' bank, founded by Renner, begins operations.

YEAR	HISTORY	CULTURE
1919	Communist Revolt in Berlin.	Thomas Hardy, *Collected Poems.*
	Paris Peace Conference adopts principle to found League of Nations.	Herman Hesse, *Demian.*
	Benito Mussolini founds Fascist movement in Italy.	George Bernard Shaw, *Heartbreak House.*
	Peace Treaty of Versailles signed.	Edward Elgar, *Concerto in E Minor for Cello.*
	Britain and France authorise resumption of commercial relations with Germany.	Film: *The Cabinet of Dr Caligari.*
	US Senate vetoes ratification of Versailles Treaty leaving US outside League of Nations.	
1920	League of Nations comes into existence.	F Scott Fitzgerald, *This Side of Paradise.*
	The Hague selected as seat of International Court of Justice.	Franz Kafka, *The Country Doctor.*
	League of Nations headquarters moves to Geneva.	Katherine Mansfield, *Bliss.*
	Bolsheviks win Russian Civil War.	Rambert School of Ballet.
	Adolf Hitler announces his 25-point programme in Munich.	
1921	Paris Conference of wartime allies fixes Germany's reparation payments.	D H Lawrence, *Women in Love.*
		Sergei Prokofiev, *The Love for Three Oranges.*
1922	League of Nations Council approves British Mandate in Palestine.	T S Eliot, *The Waste Land.*
1923	French and Belgian troops occupy the Ruhr.	P G Wodehouse, *The Inimitable Jeeves.*
	Adolf Hitler's *coup d'état* (Beer Hall Putsch) fails.	

YEAR	AGE	THE LIFE AND THE LAND
1926	56	Nov: Social Democratic Party launches radical Linz Programme.
1927	57	30 Jan: Schattendorf murders.
		15 Jul: Bloody riots in Vienna follow acquittal of Schattendorf killers.
1929	59	Dec: Constitutional amendments passed, giving the President greater powers.
1931	61	Failed customs union project between Austria and Germany.
		Apr: Renner becomes Speaker of the Nationalrat.
		May: Collapse of the Creditanstalt precipitates fall of government.
		Sep: Failed putsch attempt by Styrian *Heimwehr*.
1932	62	Apr: Austrian Nazis make good showing at provincial elections.
		15 Jul: Dollfuss guaranteed League of Nations loan in Lausanne.
1933	63	4 Mar: Parliamentary democracy comes to an end in Austria.
		20 May: Dollfuss launches Fatherland Front.

YEAR	HISTORY	CULTURE
1926	Germany admitted to League of Nations; Spain leaves as result.	A A Milne, *Winnie the Pooh*. Film: *The General*.
1927	Inter-Allied military control of Germany ends. Hitler's *Mein Kampf* published.	Virginia Woolf, *To the Lighthouse*. Film: *The Jazz Singer*.
1929	Germany accepts Young Plan at Reparations Conference in the Hague: Allies agree to evacuate Rhineland. Wall Street Crash	Erich Maria Remarque, *All Quiet on the Western Front*. Noel Coward, *Bittersweet*.
1931	National Government formed in Britain. Britain abandons Gold Standard. Nazi leader Adolf Hitler and Alfred Hugenberg of German National Party agree to co-operate. Bankruptcy of German Danatbank leads to closure of all German banks.	Noel Coward, *Cavalcade*. William Faulkner, *Sanctuary*. Architecture: Empire State Building, New York. Films: *Dracula. Little Caesar*.
1932	Chancellor Heinrich Brüning declares Germany cannot and will not resume reparation payments. Franklin D Roosevelt wins US Presidential election.	Aldous Huxley, *Brave New World*. King George V broadcasts first Royal Christmas Day message on BBC radio. Films: *Grand Hotel. Tarzan the Ape Man*.
1933	Adolf Hitler appointed Chancellor of Germany. Germany withdraws from League of Nations and Disarmament Conference.	George Orwell, *Down and Out in Paris and London*. Films: *Duck Soup. King Kong. Queen Christina*.

YEAR	AGE	THE LIFE AND THE LAND
1934	64	12–15 Feb: Civil war – Renner imprisoned for three months.
		1 May: New, 'corporate' constitution introduced.
		25 Jul: Failed putsch by Austrian Nazis – Dollfuss killed.
1936	66	Jul: Agreement signed between Germany and Austria.
1938	68	Feb: Schuschnigg summoned by Hitler to Berchtesgaden.
		12 Mar: Anschluss.
		3 Apr: Renner's interview published in which he expresses support for Anschluss.
1943	73	30 Oct: Moscow Declaration by Allies expresses desire for independent Austria after the War.

YEAR	HISTORY	CULTURE
1934	Germany: 'Night of the Long Knives'; role of German President and Chancellor merged, Hitler becomes *Führer* after German President Paul von Hindenburg dies. USSR admitted to League of Nations.	F Scott Fitzgerald, *Tender Is the Night.* Robert Graves, *I, Claudius.* Film: *David Copperfield.*
1936	German troops occupy Rhineland. Mussolini proclaims Rome-Berlin Axis.	J M Keynes, *General Theory of Employment, Interest and Money.* Berlin Olympics. Film: *Modern Times.*
1938	Munich Agreement hands Sudetenland to Germany. Kristallnacht in Germany: Jewish houses, synagogues and schools burnt for whole week.	Graham Greene, *Brighton Rock.* Evelyn Waugh, *Scoop.* Films: *Pygmalion. Alexander Nevsky. The Adventures of Robin Hood.*
1943	Second World War: Beleaguered Romanians and Germans surrender to Russians at Stalingrad. Axis forces in North Africa surrender. Italy surrenders unconditionally.	Richard Rogers and Oscar Hammerstein, *Oklahoma!* Jean-Paul Sartre, *The Flies.* Film: *For Whom the Bell Tolls. Bataan.*

YEAR	AGE	THE LIFE AND THE LAND
1945	75	30 Mar: Soviet forces take Vienna.
		Apr: Renner meets with Soviet authorities and is subsequently chosen by Stalin to form government.
		Sep: Western Allies recognise Renner government.
		20 Dec: Renner becomes first President of the Second Republic.
1950	80	14 Dec: Renner's 80th birthday – celebrations all over Austria.
		30 Dec: Renner dies.

YEAR	HISTORY	CULTURE
1945	Second World War: Mussolini shot; body displayed in Milan. Germans surrender on Italian front. Hitler commits suicide in Berlin; city surrenders to Soviets. VE Day: 8 May. US drops atomic bombs on Hiroshima and Nagasaki: Japan surrenders to Allies.	George Orwell, *Animal Farm.* Evelyn Waugh, *Brideshead Revisited.* Films: *Brief Encounter. The Way to the Stars.*
1950	Korean War breaks out. West Germany joins Council of Europe.	Ezra Pound, *Seventy Cantos.* Film: *Sunset Boulevard.*

Further Reading

A good introduction to modern Austrian history is Barbara Jelavich's *Modern Austria, Empire and Republic, 1815–1986* (Cambridge University Press, Cambridge: 1987). For a comprehensive study of 19th-century Austria it would be hard to better C A Macartney's colossal *The Habsburg Empire 1790–1918* (Weidenfeld and Nicholson, London: 1968). Those who prefer their history in smaller, spicier portions might like to try A J P Taylor's *The Habsburg Monarchy 1809–1918* (Penguin, London: 1990), which serves up a very digestible read, complete with a side order of the author's trademark biting wit. Alan Sked's *The Decline and Fall of the Habsburg Empire 1815–1918* (Longman, London: 1989) and Robin Okey's *The Habsburg Monarchy c1765–1918: From Enlightenment to Eclipse* (Macmillan, Basingstoke: 2001) are two other histories of 19th-century Austria that come highly recommended. Robert Kann's two-volume *The Multinational Empire: Nationalism and National Reform in the Habsburg Monarchy 1848–1918* (Octagon Books, New York: 1977), meanwhile, is an excellent introduction to all the different nationalities in the Monarchy, as well as the constitutional reforms of the later 19th century which aimed at resolving national conflict. Kann has also written a survey of the empire from the 16th century until its collapse: *A History of the Habsburg Empire 1526–1918* (University of California Press, Berkley: 1974)

The material from Renner's early life has chiefly been taken from his own memoir, *An der Wende zweier Zeiten: Lebenserinnerungen von Karl Renner, Vol I* (Danubia Verlag, Vienna: 1946). For all the caution that should be reserved for autobiographical works as primary sources, this is a well-written, informative read, and it is a shame that Renner never got round to writing the other three volumes he had originally planned. No biography of Renner exists in English; the two modern ones that have been used for this study are Walter Rauscher's *Karl Renner: Ein österreichischer Mythos* (Ueberreuter, Vienna: 1995), and the volume edited by Siegfried Nasko and Johannes Reichl for the Renner Museum in his former villa in Gloggnitz: *Karl Renner: Zwischen Anschluß und Europa* (Verlag Holzhausen, Vienna: 2000). The Rauscher book is factually exhaustive and a very useful source, but its historical material is not put in adequate context. The Nasko and Reichl volume is a thematic rather than chronological treatment of Renner's life, quirkily written and nicely balancing a wealth of anecdotal material with more serious analysis. Siegfried Nasko has also edited a compilation of Renner's letters and other people's memories of him, entitled *Karl Renner in Dokumenten und Erinnerungen* (Österreichischer Bundesverlag, Vienna: 1982). The assortment of letters reproduced here is so selective, however, that its usefulness is limited.

There is scant material on the Treaty of St Germain in German, let alone in English. Alfred Low's *The Anschluss Movement 1918–1919 and the Paris Peace Conference*

(American Philosophical Society, Philadelphia: 1974) is a forensic but highly readable study of its subject, and contains a good deal of information about the Conference, albeit mainly restricted to Anschluss. It is also fairly quiet about the differences between Bauer and Renner on the issue. Margaret MacMillan's excellent *Peacemakers: The Paris Conference of 1919 and Its Attempt to End War* (John Murray, London: 2001) has little material specifically on Austria, but what she does write is incisive and highly entertaining. By contrast, the letters of Franz Klein compiled by Fritz Fellner, *Saint-Germain im Sommer 1919: Die Briefe Franz Kleins aus der Zeit seiner Mitwirkung in der österreichischen Friedensdelgation. Mai–August 1919, Quellen zur Geschichte des 19. und 20. Jahrhunderts, Band 1* (Verlag Wolfgang Neugebauer, Salzburg: 1977), paint a gloomy picture of the Austrians' time in Paris from a very personal perspective. They represent, however, the most detailed account of that summer from an Austrian perspective.

Literature in English on post-imperial Austria is relatively thin on the ground. In an attempt to rectify this, a group of scholars have put together a collection of accessible essays looking at different episodes in the country's 20th-century history. The result is Rudolf Steininger, Günter Bischof and Michael Gehler (eds), *Austria in the Twentieth Century* (Transaction Publishers, New Brunswick and London: 2002). The most comprehensive study on inter-war Austria in English is Charles Gulick's mammoth, two-volume *Austria from Habsburg to Hitler* (University of California Press, Berkley and Los Angeles, 1948), which makes no attempt to disguise its heavy bias towards the Social Democratic Party. Its sheer length and attention to detail will probably defeat all but the most zealous student of Austria. A much shorter and more recent work is Francis Carsten's *The First Austrian Republic 1918–1938* (Gower, Cambridge: 1986) which is maybe better as a reference rather than a narrative history of the period. It is particularly good on the *Heimwehr*, about which Carsten has elsewhere written in more detail. Alfred Low's *The Anschluss Movement, 1931–1938, and the Great Powers* (East European Monographs, Boulder: 1985) is a follow-up to his earlier work listed above. Although again this is a specialist study, the Anschluss issue was so central to inter-war Austria that the book offers a wider insight than a monograph might suggest. Klemens von Klemperer's *Ignaz Seipel: Christian Statesman in a Time of Crisis* (Princeton University Press, Princeton: 1972), meanwhile, is an interesting and well-written biography of the dominant political figure in 1920s Austria.

George Gedye's *Fallen Bastions: The Central European Tragedy* (Victor Gollancz, London: 1939) is a beautifully written classic, peppering an informed historical account of inter-war Austria with his own, often witty, eyewitness reports from 1927 onwards as Central European correspondent for *The Times*. Gordon Brook-Shepherd's *The Austrians: A Thousand-Year Odyssey* (Harper Collins, London: 1996), in contrast to Gedye's left-leaning perspective, shows striking sympathy for the Dollfuss regime and Austrian conservatism in general. The book surveys the whole of Austria's history, but two-thirds is devoted to the 20th century and it contains some real gems within the well-crafted narrative. Kurt von Schuschnigg's vivid and atmospheric account of the last days of Austrian independence is also in English translation: *Austrian Requiem* (Victor Gollancz, London: 1947).

Robert Keyserlingk's *Austria in WWII: An Anglo-American Dilemma* (McGill-Queen's University Press, Kingston and Montreal: 1988) takes an Allied perspective and examines the wartime plans for a future independent Austria. Giles MacDonogh's *After the Reich: From the Liberation of Vienna to the Berlin Airlift* (John Murray, London: 2007) focuses on the experiences of the German nation in the aftermath of the war and traces some fascinating personal stories. A volume of scholarly essays edited by Kurt Richard Luther and Peter Pulzer, *Austria 1945–95: Fifty Years of the Second Republic* (Ashgate, Aldershot: 1998), considers the political developments in the post-war period and also looks at the changing nature of Austrian identity.

Picture Sources

The author and publishers wish to express their thanks to the following sources of illustrative material and/or permission to reproduce it. They will make proper acknowledgements in future editions in the event that any omissions have occurred.

Endpapers
The Signing of Peace in the Hall of Mirrors, Versailles, 28th June 1919 by Sir William Orpen (Imperial War Museum: Bridgeman Art Library)
Front row: Dr Johannes Bell (Germany) signing with Herr Hermann Müller leaning over him
Middle row (seated, left to right): General Tasker H Bliss, Col E M House, Mr Henry White, Mr Robert Lansing, President Woodrow Wilson (United States); M Georges Clemenceau (France); Mr David Lloyd George, Mr Andrew Bonar Law, Mr Arthur J Balfour, Viscount Milner, Mr G N Barnes (Great Britain); Prince Saionji (Japan)

Back row (left to right): M Eleftherios Venizelos (Greece);
Dr Afonso Costa (Portugal); Lord Riddell (British Press);
Sir George E Foster (Canada); M Nikola Pašić (Serbia);
M Stephen Pichon (France); Col Sir Maurice Hankey,
Mr Edwin S Montagu (Great Britain); the Maharajah of
Bikaner (India); Signor Vittorio Emanuele Orlando (Italy);
M Paul Hymans (Belgium); General Louis Botha (South
Africa); Mr W M Hughes (Australia)

Jacket images

(Front): Imperial War Museum: akg Images.
(Back): *Peace Conference at the Quai d'Orsay* by Sir William
Orpen (Imperial War Museum: akg Images).
Left to right (seated): Signor Orlando (Italy); Mr Robert
Lansing, President Woodrow Wilson (United States); M
Georges Clemenceau (France); Mr David Lloyd George, Mr
Andrew Bonar Law, Mr Arthur J Balfour (Great Britain);
Left to right (standing): M Paul Hymans (Belgium); Mr
Eleftherios Venizelos (Greece); The Emir Feisal (The
Hashemite Kingdom); Mr W F Massey (New Zealand);
General Jan Smuts (South Africa); Col E M House (United
States); General Louis Botha (South Africa); Prince Saionji
(Japan); Mr W M Hughes (Australia); Sir Robert Borden
(Canada); Mr G N Barnes (Great Britain); M Ignacy
Paderewski (Poland)

Index

Makers
of the
Modern
World

UK PUBLICATION: November 2008 to December 2010
CLASSIFICATION: Biography/History/
    International Relations
FORMAT: 198 × 128mm
EXTENT: 208pp
ILLUSTRATIONS: 6 photographs plus 4 maps
TERRITORY: world

Chronology of life in context, full index, bibliography innovative layout
with sidebars